Communicating
with Animals

Communicating with Animals

The Spiritual Connection Between People and Animals

Arthur Myers

CB
CONTEMPORARY BOOKS

Library of Congress Cataloging-in-Publication Data

Myers, Arthur.
    Communicating with animals: the spiritual connection between
people and animals / Arthur Myers.
       p.   cm.
    Includes index.
    ISBN 0-8092-3149-2
    1. Human-animal communication.   I. Title.
QL776.M94   1997
133.8'2—dc20   96-44650
                                                     CIP

Cover design by Kim Bartko
Cover photograph: Copyright © David B. Sutton
Interior design and production by Robin Stearns

Published by Contemporary Books
A division of NTC/Contemporary Publishing Group, Inc.
4255 West Touhy Avenue, Lincolnwood (Chicago), Illinois 60712-1975 U.S.A.
Printed in the United States of America
International Standard Book Number: 0-8092-3149-2
      02 03 04 ML 21 20 19 18 17 16 15 14 13 12 11 10 9 8 7 6 5

To Bob Leroy and Velsa Watterson
—a couple of Miracles workers

Contents

Preface

S ome of the concepts in this book may be hard to accept. I am fully
aware of this because I am a skeptic myself. But my skepticism, I
like to think, is positive rather than negative. I am willing to
maintain an open mind—even, in fact, do some investigating.

When I first heard of communication with animals I thought it might
be possible—but only by a gifted mystic. As I began to research this
book I heard over and over that *anyone* is potentially able to do it, anyone who is willing to work at it and suspend disbelief.

Some years ago I began a series of books on ghosts and hauntings. By
the time I had investigated a few dozen cases, I was almost certain that
there *are* ghosts—the spirits of people who have made the transition we
call death—and that there are other dimensions all around us, perhaps
even in us, that do not ordinarily register on our limited five senses, but
are there nevertheless and can be tapped into.

I sometimes feel that the most meaningful praise I ever received for
these endeavors came from a professor at the Massachusetts Institute of
Technology who was visiting the home of friends of mine. My friends
had some of my ghost books on their shelves, and the professor mentioned that he had one of my books. His hosts commented that they

were surprised that an MIT professor would be reading such far-out material. He replied, "That guy's books are all through MIT. He writes books about ghosts for people who don't believe in ghosts."

I presume he meant that I beat the bushes for witnesses, speak with people who seem to be provably psychic—as far as such things can be proved—and build as extensive a collection of pertinent information as possible.

I began my working life as an investigative reporter for newspapers and won prizes at it. I feel that I am still an investigative reporter, although my subjects are more outré now than they were at the beginning of my career.

William of Occam was an English philosopher of the thirteenth century who gave his name to the idea that when considering explanations for a puzzling question it is best to choose the simplest, most apparent answer. His theory has for centuries been called Occam's razor.

I have my own version of Occam's razor. I usually lean toward the answer that is not only the simplest and most apparent, but also the most interesting, the most fun.

I hope you have fun reading this book.

Communicating
with Animals

1

You Can Talk with Animals if You're Psychic— and We're All Psychic

C an you talk with animals?

I don't mean, can you say, "Sit, Rover" or "Let's play ball" and get an appropriate response from your four-legged friend. Anyone who has dealt with domesticated animals knows that such communication is possible, that the animals can understand some things you say.

They don't talk back, of course, although there is the occasional responsive bark or meow, or body language such as scratching on the door to be let out, or sitting by a food dish as a hint that it's time to eat.

But can you *hear* from them? Can you go into their minds, can you know what they are thinking and feeling? Can you carry on a two-way, intelligent conversation with them?

The answer is yes.

The first time such a notion crossed my essentially conventional consciousness was when I heard a public talk by a young woman named Nancy Regalmuto, who is a professional psychic and whose chief clientele is animals, especially racehorses. She had built a nationwide reputation among horse people, particularly proprietors of racing stables.

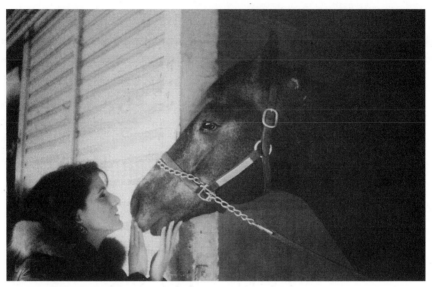

Nancy Regalmuto encouraging a client

These are very practical, realistic, hard-nosed folk. To get their attention—and to get paid by them—you've got to do what you say you can do. Nancy could find hairline fractures in horses' legs that x-rays couldn't detect. She could see them psychically. She could communicate telepathically with animals and ascertain their emotional problems, and the reasons for their actions—for example, why a horse wasn't trying to win.

In her lecture she told of a young horse who had started a promising career but who then seemed to be doing everything she could to lose. The horse might have been angry, she might have been sad, but she obviously was never up for the race. Nancy went to the stable and had a chat with the reluctant filly, who told a sad tale. She had been torn from her mother's side and sent to a strange stable. Her only tie to her familiar life was a battered old feed bucket. It was like the comforting blue blanket of Linus, the little boy in the comic strip "Peanuts."

With this bucket as her consolation, the young horse was able to function, to earn her daily hay. But one day the stables were painted. The old bucket was snatched away and a gleaming new bucket was substituted. The lonely horse's spirit could not handle this. She moped in her stall and lagged on the track. She told Nancy the reason for her distress, and when the sympathetic psychic passed this on to the owners, they resurrected the old bucket. The filly perked up and began to win.

The person who had sponsored the lecture, Tom C'sere of Southbridge, Massachusetts, gave me some additional startling information. He told me that many people across the country were communicating with animals, that it was a movement that had, in the past ten years, been quietly exploding.

I began to investigate and found that there are thousands of people who are now doing such communication. I discovered a highly intriguing aspect of the phenomenon—it largely involves people who lay no claim to psychic, mystical powers. They are just ordinary folks.

The operative truth is that *all* of us ordinary folks are psychic. We have just forgotten our powers somewhere along the way. But we can remember them. And this book is an account of my wanderings among these mostly ordinary people—the number of which is growing with startling rapidity—people who are discovering their closeness to and ability to reach the consciousness of animals, as well as other aspects of nature with which we humans share this planet, such as trees, plants, rocks, and the earth itself.

It's part of the oneness of the universe that we are becoming aware of at this moment just before the dawn of the twenty-first century, this morning of the Aquarian Age.

2

The Plight of
Robbie the Cockatoo

I began my research for this book on April 1, 1995. The first person I interviewed was twenty-eight-year-old Sean Ebnet of Bellingham, Washington, one of the comparatively few males practicing animal communication, although the number is growing. As in most other psychic/spiritual pursuits, the majority of practitioners and devotees are women. Women, it appears, are closer to earth and to heaven. Where does that leave us men?

At one point in our interview, Sean mentioned that in working with animals one quickly becomes aware that animals have had past lives, and that they remember them. This was a stopper for me. The thought flashed through my mind that this day was April Fool's Day. Could he be kidding me? But in succeeding months, as I went from one communicator to another, I found that they almost all professed the same awareness. This was the first of a series of surprises in store for me.

Sean Ebnet is not *quite* as ordinary a person as I'd like for my first interviewee in this book. I put him so high up in the story—as newspaper people say—because of the fetching April Fool's Day angle. Sean's mother, Jacqueline Snyder, is a well-known psychic. She speaks, teaches, and does psychic readings on a number of continents. Sean told

Sean Ebnet

me, "My mother, you should write a book about her. We hardly ever see her anymore; she's really on the fast track."

Sean disclaims any unique, built-in abilities, although he admits that growing up with a psychic mother didn't hurt. "I don't want to indicate a sort of fallout effect," he says, "but you can't help but be influenced when you're exposed to things like that. I don't think I was more gifted than anybody else. I just think I had more interest in it. *All* people have psychic ability. Most people did it quite often when they were children. We get away from it when we get older. In school, children are moved to more of an analytical, left-brain mode of thinking. I think that as children most people are very visual. They can communicate telepathically, although they don't realize it. It comes from connecting with your own inner abilities, connecting to the one source. Some people call it God."

Sean was aware of animal communication as a teenager, and at some level he hoped later to practice it. "But," he says, "I felt that getting a scientific education would give me a little more credibility." He earned a degree in zoology at the University of Washington, and for a time he worked in zoos. But for a person who was acutely aware of the animals' emotions and thoughts, such work was difficult. "The emotional stuff that goes on in zoos can be pretty bad," he says. "Often the animals have a great deal of rage." So he became a fish and wildlife biologist, a profession he still practices, alternating this work with his animal communication. When he was apprenticing as a communicator, he often worked with Samantha Khury, an experienced, highly regarded practitioner in the field. Of that time in his life, Sean told me:

The case I remember best involved a cockatoo. It was in San Diego, three years ago.

I was beginning to have doubts about what I was doing. I was at a point where I'd have a good session and then I wouldn't have a good session. I was getting frustrated. I wanted to become more visual; I wanted to be more able to see what the animal was thinking, what was in its mind. The universe, I think, picked up on that.

The next session I had was with a bird named Robbie. Robbie had pulled out all of his feathers. He was staying with Samantha. He belonged to a man who had worked with her husband. I didn't know what the situation was at the time, but I knew the bird was supposed to eventually go back to his owner. I was at Samantha's house and she suggested that I work with Robbie. So I went into the room where she had him and began to work with him, to try to reach his mind and emotions.

The first thing I heard was water. At first I thought it was the ocean. It was big, and through the eyes of the bird I could see a lot of people around. Robbie was on this man's shoulder. The man was dark complexioned, but not necessarily Mexican. There are a lot of Mexicans in that area. This man had dark hair, but a different facial structure from a Hispanic person.

Then I got a different sound, like a waterfall. Robbie liked that sound. I could feel that it was very soothing to him. You get a picture, and then you feel the emotion, whatever the animal is feeling, whether they like the feeling, or if they don't. This sound was very important to Robbie, and he wasn't getting it anymore. He hadn't heard the water for a long time, and he was upset about that. He also showed me what the house he had lived in looked like. It had very dark, dark wood paneling. His cage was away from the window, and he wasn't comfortable with that.

Then I saw this man walking back and forth in the house. It was the same man I had seen at the beach, with Robbie on his shoulder.

Samantha Khury with a large friend

There was something odd about this man. He would walk back and forth and not even acknowledge Robbie. And I could feel that Robbie was very devoted to this man, very emotional toward him. The man would walk around, back and forth, making hand gestures, kind of crazy.

And Robbie was thinking that if he acted crazy himself, the man might notice him. So the bird began pulling its feathers out. The bird would bob his head up and down and make screeching noises to get this person's attention. But it didn't work. And it was like the bird was saying, "It's him, but it's not him." Some people might feel that animals don't know words like this, that they don't understand language, but I definitely was getting that phrase—"It's him, but it's not him." It was so clear that I wrote it down.

I told Samantha what I had gotten, and she said this was very good. And she told me what was going on with the bird. She said this bird belonged to a man whose name was Ben. Ben had owned Robbie all of the bird's life. And Ben was Filipino, that was the dark complexion and the different facial structure. He wasn't Hispanic, as I hadn't felt he was, but he was not Caucasian. I asked Samantha about the beach, and she said that Robbie and Ben went everywhere together. It was a very close relationship.

I asked her about the waterfall, and she didn't know what that was. I asked her about the words I had heard from the bird—"It's him, but it's not him." Then she told me that Ben was suffering from a mental disease, and that he would get into phases when he didn't recognize the bird, or even seem to see it. And for Robbie this was extremely traumatic.

Later that day, we were supposed to take the bird back to Ben's house. Ben had gotten some treatment and was back home. His mother was now staying there. When we got there, I saw a big fountain in front of the house and I knew that was what I had gotten the sound of water from. The fountain was broken, and had been for a while. And inside the house, sure enough, it was very dark. Ben's mother, it turned out, had moved Robbie's cage from near the window, because she was afraid he would be too hot in the sun. She had moved the cage back into the darkest part of the house, where it was cooler, but to the bird this was very upsetting.

After that session, I felt much more confident and my sessions got a lot better. You get that faith and you become much better.

———————

I spoke several weeks later with Sean's mother, Jacqueline Snyder, who travels the world lecturing and observing, and she gave me some thoughts that underscore some of the general concepts that I was running across in my research for this book. She told me:

This is the most exciting time of the planet. I think we are in probably the most important decade in the history of humanity. There is so much assistance coming to people, and so much going on inside their own individual psyches. I've met so many—doctors, lawyers, military people—they're all feeling something. That something has everything to do with the light that came to me ten years ago, and what my work and many other people's work is about. And that is helping people understand that feeling, giving them tools to go deeper in understanding how they can be more participatory in making a more unified and loving race of people.

This takes me into all cultures, and definitely into Native American. My mother was Cherokee. There is an earth wisdom that is carried by indigenous people to help the rest of us come back into that knowledge.

I think the negativity that has been communicated for so long on Earth is playing out. I think the awakening is starting already, and is escalating. Critical mass is approaching and we will move quickly to the point that will bring everyone with us.

3

How People Get Started Chatting with Animals

While I was in full struggle with this book, I had dinner one evening in Boston with a writer friend named Irene Briskin. She was intrigued when I told her I was writing a book about communication with animals, and she informed me that she constantly communicated with her cat, Nitzchka.

Nitzchka, Irene told me, had originally belonged to a Lithuanian filmmaker who was moving from Boston. "I mentioned that I didn't have a cat," Irene said, "and she came around that evening with Nitzchka. She said, 'Here she is, good-bye.'"

Nitzchka, which means "night" in Lithuanian, was six months old when Irene had acquired her seventeen years before. She was a cat who really bonded with people. That memorable first evening, she went around howling for her former owner. But soon she became very attached to Irene and her son. Irene's son grew up, became a psychiatrist, got married, moved to Baltimore, and took Nitzchka with him. After all, he'd known her most of his life.

"She's still alive," Irene said, "although she has arthritis. But my son is medicating her. Now she can do everything but climb a tree."

This struck me as a very sweet story. And if Irene could really talk with Nitzchka it would be a marvelous touch for the book, for Irene had not taken any training in communication with animals; she was just an ordinary cat owner. I got so excited that I urged her not to tell me any more in the din of the restaurant, since I did not have a tape recorder or even paper and pencil. I'd call her the next morning under proper conditions, with my trusty recorder plugged into my phone, and get every word of the story. "OK," she said, and the next morning she told me about Nitzchka.

"Nitzchka developed what I call speech," Irene said. "She developed intonation. The first night I had her, I spoke to her a good deal, she was so bereaved. She would keep up a wailing and a caterwauling. She'd search all over the place for her friend the filmmaker. She began answering me. If I asked a question, she would answer with the intonation of an answer, in which I could imagine words."

"Were you doing anything telepathic?" I asked Irene.

"No," she replied, "I didn't think it was anything telepathic at all. But another interesting thing that developed is that she liked to sit on the doorstep and when people went by she greeted them. One out of four people understood immediately, stopped, and spoke back to her. And then she would have a long conversation. She would keep up a continuing meowing, up and down, and hardly ever repeating the same thing. She had learned to imitate some of our human intonations."

A cute story, but for me it was a disappointing start to the day. Irene hadn't realized what I meant by animal communication. I wasn't planning a book about vague mewing noises made by a warmhearted, congenial cat. I'd love to meet Nitzchka and have an exchange of intonations, but that wasn't what I was looking for that morning. I was going for broke when it came to animal communication. I expressed my disappointment as gently as I could.

However, as we closed our conversation, Irene said something that from my point of view was quite pertinent. She said that she sometimes seems able to communicate psychically with animals. Most people are very cagey about admitting such things. In our society, we are so bludgeoned into the left-brain mode of thinking that it's not considered cool to speak of such things.

For example, I recall interviewing a thirteen-year-old girl who figured in a chapter of one of my ghost books. She had a twin sister who had died in infancy and who now seemed to be growing up with her, as evidenced by poltergeist phenomena—rappings, disappearance and movement of the living girl's possessions, and so on. I asked the girl if she were psychic, and she denied this. But as we talked, she realized that I considered psychic ability a gift, not something weird. Before long, she was telling me that she and her girlfriend in school could, as she put it, call each other with their minds.

"We can give each other messages," she said. "She'll be sitting across the room in class, and I'll call her with my mind and she'll look."

People are so prone to act the way they are expected to act, encouraged to act. So I was pleasantly surprised when Irene told me, "I can communicate enough to wish a cat to turn around and come and talk to me in the street, and it does. And so do birds. When I don't get a good chance to look at a bird, I say in my mind, 'Oh turn around and come back.' And it often circles around and does just that."

It occurs to me that we may all be on the edge of telepathic communication. It is said that people who live close to the earth, away from the helter-skelter of modern life, people such as the Australian Aborigines, regard telepathic communication as routine.

So I suspect that my chat with Irene about Nitzchka was not a morning's jaunt down the wrong road. It may be a road we're all traveling without even being aware of it. Very possibly Nitzchka was aware of it, and was consciously reading Irene's mind, as well as those of passersby in the street.

Smart cat. But then we're probably *all* smart cats, smarter than we realize.

How do people get into consciously telepathic communication with animals? Some people are aware of their ability to communicate telepathically from early childhood. For others, it comes on gradually. An intriguing example of the latter is a young man named Sam Louie, of Berkeley, California. Sam told me he was currently working part-time as an animal communicator but was hoping to develop it into a full-time occupation.

"What do you do full-time?" I asked.

"You won't believe this, but I'm a lawyer," he replied. "I'm hoping to transition out of the law life, like every other lawyer that exists."

(I might mention, for whatever significance it might have, that this was during the height—or depth—of the O. J. Simpson trial.)

"You mean all lawyers want to get out of law?" I asked.

"Well, maybe not all, but a high percentage. It usually happens about the fifth week of law school."

I asked him how he had realized he was psychic, and he laughed.

"It started in picking juries, I guess. I was able to figure out what some of the jurors were going to say before they said it. During jury selection, the judge would ask the jurors whether they had been victims of crime, and I started picking up on what people had been victimized by. A juror would say, 'I was the victim of a shooting incident,' and I would pick up on that before the juror said it."

Sam is a public defender who works in public-interest law. He seems something of an idealist. When I asked him if he used his newfound psychic abilities in his law practice, he said, "I do pick up things during a trial, but basically I don't use my psychic skills in court. I don't think that's fair to my opponent."

Will wonders never cease!

Sam is a dog lover, and he soon realized that he was able to use his gift with his own dog and with others. He volunteered to work with a Doberman Rescue League in his area and was off on a new career.

But many communicators started out simply as animal lovers, people who had run out of gas with conventional veterinarians and who turned to less customary practitioners. Judy Meyer made a phone call one day, and it changed her life. Judy, a sculptor, lives in a small town in New Mexico called Tesuque, near Santa Fe. From early childhood she has been a dedicated animal lover. She has seven cats and an Alaskan malamute.

With all those animals, Judy has had her share of problems. One was Chat Gris, a cat she had owned for all his thirteen years. During all that time Chat Gris had never once used the litter box. No veterinarian had been able to solve this perplexing, understandably annoying mystery. Then Judy heard of a woman named Penelope Smith, who lived in Point Reyes, California. Penelope is possibly the best known of animal communicators today. She has trained hundreds of people in the art—or science—of animal communication. These people often have gone on to train others. Penelope is at the epicenter of the animal communication movement.

"A friend told me about a woman in California who could talk to animals," Judy told me. "I said, 'That's nice,' and blew it off. I thought, That's

Sam Louie and his cat, Frito Man

a dream come true. I would love to know what they think, but that's not real. But Chat Gris's lifelong aversion to the litter box was becoming too much. I called this woman, who was Penelope Smith. We did a consultation on the phone."

Incidentally, many communicators prefer to work over the phone. Animal communication can apparently be done at any distance. One communicator, Tim Beihoff, who lives in Sussex, Wisconsin, and whose specialty is finding missing animals, told me of finding two lost cats in Prague, Czechoslovakia, without leaving his home. The advantage of working at a distance rather than in the presence of the animal, communicators say, is that the animal is not distracted by smells, other animals, or by the communicator.

The communicator gets on the phone with the animal's owner—or the animal's person, which is the more politically correct term in these circles. The animal need not be with its person or even nearby. The communicator can establish psychic contact with the animal no matter where it is. He or she can then carry on a telepathic conversation with the animal and discuss matters on the phone with the animal's person.

"Penelope and I did a consultation on the phone," Judy recalled. "She was accurate about my relationship with this cat and in her description of my house and the land here. Penelope said that the cat was telling her that he was too sensitive to use the litter. It was like scraping nails on a blackboard would be for us. Penelope said to put sand in the litter.

"So I went out and got a bucket of sand from my arroyo—which is Western talk for a dry streambed. I brought in the sand and mixed it into the litter box. I didn't put the cat in the box. I said, 'The woman on the phone told me what you told her. I've done what you requested. Now I'm asking you to pee in the litter.'

"He looked at me and he looked at the box, and he stepped over the edge, and he sat down, and he peed. He was thirteen, and he hadn't peed in the litter for thirteen years.

"I went, 'Oh God, this works! This is phenomenal!'

"I sat down and wrote a list of sixteen questions, involving all the cats and the dog. I called Penelope back and went over everybody. And overnight any behavioral problems I had had, any strange behavior, everything changed. Because I could now hear, through Penelope, what my animals really wanted."

Judy Meyer and friend

Judy invited Penelope Smith to come to Santa Fe and give a workshop. She and a number of other people took it. In the years since then, Judy has worked professionally as an animal communicator, doing diagnoses and sometimes healings.

She is married to a physician. "I've had hundreds of letters from people whose animals I have helped," she says, "but my husband still says that he doesn't believe this is going on. Actually, he is very psychic, much more than I am. He can hear the animals better than I can. But he's in denial. Things like this can be very threatening to people's belief systems."

After straightening out Chat Gris's problem with the litter box, Judy zeroed in on another of her cats, Teal, a dainty little blue point Siamese. Judy told me:

I have a cat room. It's off the kitchen. It's got a microwave, a refrigerator, a cat door, a cat sink, a toilet to go with the litter boxes. It's very functional. When I would go in there, Teal would look at the food I'd put down, take two steps back and run away like bloody murder, like I was trying to poison her. When I got on the phone with Penelope for the second time, I asked, "What does Teal really want to eat?" I had assumed I was not feeding her something that she really wanted. Penelope answered, "This is what Teal just said: 'Thank goodness that you asked this question.' Teal said she is totally disgusted with the amount of food you are feeding her and the other cats. She says the other cats are pigs, and she does not want to eat in that room. She says she wants one small mouthful of food in a little bowl, outside of that room."

I went, OK. I hadn't seen this cat eat in six years, since I'd had her. I knew she must be eating, because she wasn't dead. I figured she must

Penelope Smith and a llama called Raindance; photo by Marty Knapp

be eating dry food in the middle of the night when no one was in there. I got a little teeny piece of canned cat food and I put it in a bowl, and I put it down in front of Teal. And she ate!

And she was right—the rest of my cats *are* pigs.

───────────

Many people who are aware of their psychic abilities gained that knowledge early in life. They were children who didn't know that in our society you're not supposed to be able to do things like this.

An example is a friend of mine, a powerfully spiritual person who has helped me with my ghost books. Her first day in kindergarten, she relates, the children played a game with a rock. You held the rock in one hand behind your back, and the other kids tried to guess which hand held the rock. My friend quickly discovered that it's all right to guess right some of the time, but to guess right *all* of the time made people very nervous. She swept her intuitive ability under the rug until she was in her twenties, at which time she went from being a journalist to being a psychic and spiritual adviser—which I would call going from the ridiculous to the sublime.

───────────

Occasionally a person becomes psychic—or becomes *aware* of psychic proclivities—after a physical or emotional trauma. A classic example is the experience of the famous Dutch psychic Peter Hurkos. Hurkos was working as a housepainter, when at the age of twenty-two he fell four stories to the ground. When he came to, four days later in a hospital room, he began to exhibit extraordinary qualities. He screamed to his wife that their baby son was caught in a fire at home. His timing was slightly off. The child did not have his close call with fire till five days later, when he was rescued by firemen. A stranger stopped by his bed to wish Hurkos a speedy recovery, and Hurkos immediately knew the man was a British agent—this was during World War II—and that he would be killed a few days later by the Germans. As the agent left the hospital room, Hurkos screamed to stop him. Hurkos was given a sedative, and the man went unknowingly to his death. The director of the hospital taunted Hurkos, urging Hurkos to tell him something about the doctor's private life. Hurkos informed the married doctor that he had had an affair with a nurse at the hospital and that she had had a baby.

But you don't have to fall four stories to become psychic. Sometimes the ability is so firmly built in that even our conscious minds are unmistakably aware of it. A case in point is Marlene Sandler, a professional animal communicator who lives in Warrington, Pennsylvania. Marlene was aware of her communicative abilities early in life. She told me:

When I was six years old, I knew that my cousin's dog, Spotty, had a problem with his stomach. I could tell because I felt queasy in my stomach, and it wasn't *my* upset stomach; I knew it was the dog's. How did I know that? It was sudden knowing, I just knew. Nobody believed me and Spotty ended up getting real sick.

I was not in a family atmosphere that encouraged this sort of thing, so I suppressed it. Actually, my dad used to see colors and he used to send colors to me as a kid, and I'd send them back. I used to think everybody's father did that. He informed me early on that this was our little secret. My father was not comfortable with that aspect of himself. So I had a private secret world.

I became oriented to the more analytical side of myself. I went into cancer research and virological research. I did this for about ten years. So I came to the sort of work I am doing now from a very analytical background. For years I worked with electron microscopes and that sort of thing. But science didn't offer a lot of the answers, and a lot of times when we had breakthroughs it was because of dreams and intuitive kinds of stuff.

I went through a career shift, and got a master's degree in counseling from Antioch College. I've been involved in energy work for about fifteen years now. I started out doing animals as a courtesy to my human clients.

I think I came to this partially because I'm dyslexic. I don't read and write quite the same as most folks. I had midauditory minimal brain damage on the left hemisphere of my brain, and have a very highly developed right hemisphere by way of compensation. It was from being a forceps baby.

(Note: The left side of the brain is believed to govern much of the logical, down-to-earth thinking that we do; the right side influences our intuition, our creativity.)

When I was a child, they didn't know much about learning disabilities. School was not a pleasant experience for me. I used to spend most of my time looking out the window. They used to call me Cloud. I guess I spent twelve years meditating.

Marlene recalls what she considers a turning point in her life when she met a Zen master in a Philadelphia subway:

When I was twenty-five, I met a Zen master and I began redeveloping and rediscovering myself. But before I met that Zen master, when I was nineteen, I met another master in a subway station. He told me I had special gifts and that I was going to be challenged to deal with them.

We sat there and got chatting because the train was late. I thought he was weird, and I kept moving over. He was an Asian, probably around thirty-five. He had started talking to me and telling me about me. Of course, that was a fascinating subject, right? But at the same time, I felt uncomfortable. Among other things, I'm only four feet, eleven inches. I wasn't in a place where I was real comfortable with myself at that time. So I started moving over and over on the bench,

Marlene Sandler and Charlie

to the point where I was about to fall off. So I got up and walked away. He sat quietly. But I realized he was a gentle, beautiful man so I sat back down again. He had given a lecture and he was still in robes. Our conversation planted seeds. A few years later I started doing training in energy work with the other Asian healer.

I do an eclectic form of counseling. I began to do cotherapy with a number of psychotherapists. I was the last stop—the little wild medicine woman.

I've always had an affinity with animals. When I was seven, my father paid twenty-five cents for me to have a ride on a horse. I loved that horse, I felt very connected to that horse. But I've never been involved with riding horses or equestrian sports. I'm not athletic.

When I was doing cotherapy, a psychotherapist asked me if I would visit a woman and her horses. These horses were Olympic hopefuls. They were very huge, very athletic—this was a performance barn. The woman had me talk about her relationships with each of the horses. I found I was able to be aware, from the animals' point of view, of their physical problems, and that this could possibly be helpful to veterinarians in their diagnoses and treatments.

At this point Marlene studied in workshops with Jeri Ryan, a well-known communicator and trainer who is based in Oakland, California, and who gives instruction throughout the country. Marlene has also studied with Penelope Smith.

We'll talk more about Marlene's methods of working with animals in Chapter 4.

———————

For years Janet Shepherd of Haymarket, Virginia, has trained horses, competed, and taught riding. She has been involved in animal communication for a couple of years. She told me it came about like this:

The first time I absolutely knew I had talked with an animal was about two years ago, when a friend of mine was going out of town and asked me to ride her horse for her. She was showing me the horse and how to tack him up and what he did and didn't like. She was a really good mother. The horse turned around and looked me

Janet Shepherd and Frosty Christmas

in the eye and said, "Cows are . . ." and there was a pause, almost as if a foreign language was being translated, and then he said, ". . . ugly." And two seconds later my friend said, "One thing you have to be careful of is that he's terrified of cows. Sometimes the cows are up by the fence, and then he'll totally freak out."

And she went on to tell me how to handle it. And I realized that the horse had actually spoken to me. I was so thrilled I just about couldn't stand myself.

I asked Janet, "What do you think is going on?"

"I think," she replied, "that it may be that when we communicate telepathically that it's like there's a translation going on. The animal might send a picture or an emotion, but it might be translated into words that we can understand. How that happens I do not know. But I feel that some animals are actually quite verbal. Whatever is coming from them is language, or part of language. Part of my belief system is reincarnation, and I think that some animals have been in human bodies in their past. For those animals, it's quite easy."

When Marta Williams, an established communicator based in Graton, California, was just beginning to communicate with animals, her roommate was skeptical. Marta told me:

He said, "OK, if you know how to do this, tell me what your cat was doing today."

So I asked my cat, "Jenny, what were you doing today?" And she immediately showed me a picture—a telepathic communication—of her and a squirrel up on the back fence, touching noses. So I told my roommate, and he said, "Oh my God, that's exactly what they were doing!"

And I went, "Oh my God, this stuff really works!"

Then I asked Jenny what she and the squirrel were talking about. I got the answer in words and phrases, and she said she was telling the squirrel to be careful of my other cats because they were mean. And also that she and the squirrel were talking about nuts, and about the squirrel's babies. It was really cute and sweet. This was a turning point for me. I have to thank Jenny every day for being so good at communicating with me that I got it. You know, animals are really good at communicating.

Griffin Kanter of Houston, Texas, grew up with intimations of her ability to speak with animals, but she didn't pursue them seriously until adulthood, when she was diagnosed with chronic fatigue syndrome. She had been an administrator with Shell Oil Corporation. She is now a full-time practitioner of animal communication, and she also teaches the art. In her workshops, she shares with students her own personal, unusual method of accessing an ability to talk with animals:

I grew up on a farm in Iowa and was there the first twelve years of my life. My sister was seven years older than me, and we never really played together or had the same interests, so animals were my friends and playmates. I could hear them and talk with them as a young child.

After my childhood this communication stopped being a constant thing. In 1985 I came down with chronic fatigue syndrome, which drastically changed my life and made me reexamine everything about it. One thing I did in the course of therapy was read a book by Lucia Catacchinone, called *The Power of Your Other Hand*. She was an art therapist who came down with a connective tissue disease, like the writer Norman Cousins. A therapist had worked with her on drawing and writing with the left hand. She then wrote this book about using the left hand to access parts of yourself. Her focus is human. I took the technique and used it to communicate with animals.

The book is about channeling the inner wisdom of the right brain. It uses the nondominant handwriting technique. It's based on Gestalt and Jungian therapy principles that the ego is made up of many subpersonalities. You use nondominant handwriting to talk to these different selves.

I would write a question with my dominant hand—the right. (A left-handed person would reverse the process.) Then I would take the pen in my left hand, hear the response, and write it. And I used this technique to communicate with others.

I decided to try it with my animals; I always have a bunch of animals. So I sat down and wrote with my dominant hand to my dog Isaac, a poodle-terrier mix. I wrote, "Isaac, I'm going to use this technique to communicate with you." And then I put the pencil in my left hand. And when the left hand began writing I knew that it was him. I had been using the handwriting technique for six months, so I was skilled in feeling the different subtle energies of the different aspects of myself—children, adult, etc.—so when his voice came in, I knew it wasn't my own. I could feel the different energy vibration. I hear through the voice that I talk to myself with

Griffin Kanter and friend

internally, the voice that's going on in one's head. The animal's voice comes in through that voice. So I don't hear a different voice, it's still my own. But I can feel the animals' emotions and sometimes their bodily sensations. So we have conversations.

At the beginning I had to write down every word that they said or the flow would stop, but I sort of built up my muscles and now I no longer have to do that kind of writing. Now I just engage in conversation with the animal mentally, just like I would talk to a human being.

Griffin emphasizes that it's important to have a receptive mind. "Think of the positive attributes of the different species," she suggests. "Basically, I think that's sending unconditional love. And pictures can be important. I'm a very visual person so I know I'm sending pictures while I'm communicating. Emotions, pictures, bodily sensations, words are all important and can be exchanged in combinations. I believe that anyone can communicate with animals. It's just believing that you can, and giving yourself permission to do so."

Have your people get in touch with my people.
Drawing by P. Steiner; © 1995 The New Yorker Magazine, Inc.

4

Ways That Animals and Humans Exchange Information

H ow is it done, this interspecies communication?

I have asked this of communicators throughout the country, and they have given me essentially the same answers. I could quote any of forty or fifty practitioners of the art to begin this chapter. A particularly precise, reader-friendly wrap-up was furnished me by Raphaela Pope, a communicator who lives in Berkeley, California. I'll start with her. She said:

There are four ways of receiving communication:

1. Getting words or a sentence.
2. Getting mental pictures. The animal sends me pictures. If the animal is lost, for example, I can see the scenes that are in its mind, that it is seeing, and that may help in finding the animal.
3. A kinesthetic sense—having your attention drawn to one area of your own body, and feeling the animal's sensations. These sensations can be emotional as well as physical.
4. A knowingness, an intuition that comes to you.

Raphaela Pope with a happy friend

Raphaela also came up with an idea that was perhaps so obvious that no one else had mentioned it. I certainly had not thought of it. Possibly no one had considered it worth voicing, but it is an intriguing explanation of why human communication with animals seems to us so startling, so sensational that one can hear gasps of delight and/or disbelief from coast to coast. It is something so seemingly outlandish that people like me write books about it.

"We're getting messages all the time," Raphaela said, "we just don't recognize it. I think we've all been born with telepathic ability, but we've chosen to shut it down, *because people have this wonderful, incredible ability that we call speech.*

"When children begin to speak, they are so highly rewarded that it's an incredibly exciting thing. And speech *is* marvelous. So the kids begin forgetting their telepathic abilities."

Like many animal communicators, Raphaela gives workshops, among the many such gatherings that are multiplying the aware human population of the planet.

"In my workshops," she says, "I remind people, 'You were *born* with this telepathic ability. You're entitled to this facility, it's your birthright.' So we're just opening up what they already have."

This reminds me of an axiom common to many spiritual doctrines: You're already in heaven, you just don't know it. For the time being, you forgot.

It's a nice thought, anyway.

Nedda Wittels and a portrait of Echo, her longtime close friend; photo by Arthur Myers

Nedda Wittels, an animal communicator who lives in Simsbury, Connecticut, remembers vividly the first time she consciously heard words from an animal. It was her beloved horse, Echo. Nedda told me:

I was riding her. We were learning how to jump. We had gone over some fences. She loves to jump, but she was a little skeptical about what we were doing; she didn't understand how to pace herself, how to position herself. I was letting her go around and figure out what to do.

We were going over a fence, in the air, when I heard a voice say, "Oh, now I've got it."

I thought, Who said that? There was nobody else around.

As we approached the next fence it was totally different, she knew exactly what to do. From there on, she went right for the fences, aggressively. She ate them up. No reluctance, no confusion.

I may have been doing this as a kid, hearing animals. I probably was a lot more psychic than I realized. I think Echo had been speaking to me for some time, until I finally heard her speaking in my head. I had read a little book by Penelope Smith called *Animal Talk* that gives you steps you can take to start communicating with your animal. Some of the things Penelope talked about I realized I had been doing for some time, it had just come natural to me.

These steps—from Penelope's book—begin with a person spending time with the animal in a quiet place and visualizing something. Then the person sends the mental picture out to a specific point in the room. After that the person sends the picture to the animal friend's body, sometimes verbally, sometimes silently. The person does whatever it takes to get the animal's attention—calling its name, rubbing its back, letting it know of the desire for communication. Sometimes it helps to picture a simple wish such as taking a walk on the beach. The person must then open his or her mind and imagine what the animal is sending back. The final step is to accept the communication received and acknowledge it. Practicing with other questions and other animals will help.

"On that first incident," Nedda said, "I definitely heard words, but other times I get information in different forms. Sometimes I get pictures, very vivid pictures. Sometimes I get emotion, very powerful emotion.

Sometimes I get a combination of pictures and sounds. Sometimes I get a concept, I mean a kind of knowing. You suddenly have the information.

"I sometimes think that I'm tapping into a level of consciousness that to me is a level of Godness. I believe every form is an expression of God and that it contains God within it. So I'm just tapping into another layer. Otherwise, why would time and space be irrelevant? Why would I be able to be three thousand miles away and have a conversation with an animal I've never met? Or my own horse, whom I have talked to when I have been on the other side of the continent?"

―――――――――

Another communicator who spoke very usefully about how thoughts are received from animals is Betty Lewis of Amherst, New Hampshire.

"A lot of communicators," she said, "have been aware of being psychic from childhood, but I don't recall doing it in childhood. My first awareness came when I read a book by Beatrice Lydecker called *What the Animals Tell Me*. I started practicing and playing with it. It seemed like a good tool for me as a Great Dane breeder and show judge, and a veterinarian technician."

Lydecker, of North Hollywood, California, is an icon of the animal communication movement. She was one of the first communicators to come out of the closet, to acknowledge publicly that she could exchange information with animals.

"I went to a workshop with Bea," Betty said. "I don't feel that it's a special gift. I think it's a skill we all can develop, like learning another language.

"People are individuals, and I believe that the information comes to them in their own particular strength. It also comes in the animal's strength, of course, but I believe you have to speak through your own experience as a human. I think visual people tend to get more complete visions, like a movie script. I get things very strongly as far as feelings are concerned.

"I think everyone has the capacity to develop all their other senses, and that's one of the things I teach in my workshops, learning your own strengths and then concentrating on developing the others. So that over the years my visual acuity has become stronger, my olfactory information has become better. That's important when you're communicating with dogs

Betty Lewis and two very Great Danes, Liberty and Phoenix

because that's their primary sense. With auditory communication—words—I guess the reason that it doesn't come as clearly all the time is that dogs, cats, horses, and so forth don't use language the same way we do. When I communicate, sometimes words come clearly, but it's not something I rely on."

I mentioned to Betty that Sean Ebnet and some other communicators I had talked with felt that perhaps when communication comes in actual words there is an intermediary that we humans who are currently residing in bodies do not readily perceive, such as spirit guides or possibly an angel. Betty, who struck me as a very down-to-earth rural New England woman, replied, "Well I think so, too. I'm not very articulate, but during some sessions with animals I become very articulate. Words come through very easily, and I feel there is some other connection than just between the animal and me—perhaps with either the animal's guide or my guide. I don't know exactly who all the time, but it is a regular phenomenon. Suddenly the words come out of me very easily, as though they were written in a script. When the conversation is over, I go back to being me."

Raphaela Pope put the emphasis on the particular characteristics and ways of communicating of the animal. She told me:

The way it comes through often depends on the animal. For instance, if you're talking with a dog who has lived in your house for ten years, and he has a recognition vocabulary of seven or eight hundred words, this is a dog who can practically spell out the alphabet. So you may get words from him, you may actually get sentences.

On the other hand, if you're talking to an animal who hasn't spent a lot of time in the house—or a sparrow or blue jay—they probably don't have much familiarity with human speech, so what you're likely to get from them is feelings, or pictures, sometimes thoughts.

You have to have all your receptivity centers on cue, so you can get whatever is coming. You can get physical feelings as well as emotional. I just did a reading on a cat that is quite ill. I got the sensation of having a chest pressure. It turned out that the cat did indeed have a tumor in the chest wall.

Often your attention will be drawn to, or you'll have an actual sensation in, those body parts of the person or animal to whom you are talking. My first dog, Petey, was a good talker. He was very talky. An example of feeling—emotionalism—is when I was doing a consultation on a lost dog and I was just flooded with a sensation of a kind of forlornness, a sadness and confusion.

Raphaela mentioned that her husband is a professional computer person. "He's very left-brain," she said. "For a long time he reserved judgment on my doings. But now he's more and more convinced of their reality."

Constant exposure to the phenomenon does tend to make one something of a believer. I should know, having spent more than a year interviewing and observing several dozen communicators.

"People in the families of those who do psychic work," Raphaela told me, "become more and more psychic themselves all the time. They just can't help it."

A communicator from Hayward, California, who goes by the exotic name of Winterhawk had an intriguing answer for my question as to where animals might get their words. "Sometimes I call it the big computer in the sky," she said. "The big translator puts it in a language I can understand."

Winterhawk mentioned with a chuckle that her original name was ·
Liz. "The name Winterhawk," she said, "was given me by my guides
to connect me with my work and nature. It was a gift to help me get
on-purpose."

She was born in Kansas and says her folks were prairie people,
although she had an offbeat grandmother who was psychic. Winterhawk
was a bit unusual from the start. "As a child," she says, "I just considered it natural to be able to sense how others were feeling. I would tend
to interpret people as colors. I'd say, that lady's really brown, or that one
is orange. Later, I went through a part of my life when I sort of let go
of this, but then in the 1970s I did massage therapy and Reiki work.
You get a lot of sensations doing that—feelings and pictures—and I think
that developed my psychic work. Mostly I was working with people, but
a teacher told me, 'I think animals are your pathway.'

"I often hear words from the animals, but we all have different receptive channels that are open to us. Some people are very good at hearing information but not so good at seeing or feeling it. I'm very audio,
so I hear words. Sometimes animals send me poetry."

By the time I got to Winterhawk, several communicators had told me
they had received poetry from animals. The first to spring this startling
concept on me was a down-to-earth type, a former dairy farmer from
New Hampshire, who quoted me a poem from a cat. And it was a good
poem, not doggerel. I filed this information in the way-out category, to
be considered with extreme care before putting it in this book, but by
the time the fourth or fifth quite sane-sounding person told me of such
an experience I was ready to—if not necessarily believe it—at least think
about it seriously. I've devoted the last chapter of this book to poetry
from animals. I purposely chose to make it the last chapter, to give the
reader maximum time to get used to odd ideas.

Although Winterhawk may not be your next door–neighbor type, she
came up with some well-put sentiments for next door–neighbor types
who might like to communicate with animals: "Anyone can communicate who is willing to take the time to be quiet and respectful and hum-
ble enough to hear words of communication from another being. It's a
matter of quieting the mind and opening the heart. Anyone who wants
to can practice it."

As must be apparent by now, animal communication is a very individual thing. There are many different ways of doing it. Dawn Hayman is one of the best-known communicators. She is also coproprietor of Spring Farm CARES, a not-for-profit refuge for animals, situated in Clinton, New York. Dawn communicates through words, but says she doesn't actually *hear* them.

"The way I receive information is through thoughts, ideas, and feelings," she says. "I put the words to it. I don't hear words, although it can get quite specific. There are different feelings between words, like pretty and beautiful, for example. You can say, 'That person is pretty,' or, 'That person is beautiful,' but the words have different intensities. But I don't hear a voice or anything like that."

––––––––––

I asked Marlene Sandler, whom we met in the previous chapter, how she converses with animals. "I get images, impressions, and feelings," she replied. "I sense what the animal wants to convey, and then an energetic dialogue takes place. I think it comes through whatever is your dominant sense. Some people may be more kinesthetic, some more visual, some olfactoral, some auditory. I think that what comes back telepathically comes to you the way you can best decode or decipher it. Lots of times you get things that are metaphors."

I asked what she meant by metaphors. She replied, "A woman called me and told me her cats weren't eating and she was very upset about them. The first image I got when I tuned in to the cats was an empty bathtub. The words that came into my head were, 'You haven't taken a bath.' So I said to the woman, 'This is not a comment on your hygiene, but the symbol I'm getting is that you haven't taken a bath and the cats are upset about that.'

"The meaning of that, as the consultation went on, was that the woman had been in a high-stress position in her job, and she had not had time to come home and rest. Ordinarily, she would come home, take a nice, luxurious bath, the cats would play with her along the edge of the bathtub, and they would have all this playtime together. Now she was taking showers and the playtime was gone. The cats were feeling neglected, and they were also feeling her being very compressed and under stress.

"In another case, there was a cat from whom I got a symbol of an empty porch. The woman kept saying, 'We don't have a porch.' It turned out that the empty porch symbolized that the woman's brother had committed suicide. The woman and the cat had often gone to the brother's house, and he had a porch. And the porch was empty now and the cat was saddened by it."

Nedda Wittels of Simsbury, Connecticut, taught social studies and psychology in public school, as well as in adult education courses. She sometimes brought in lecturers to talk about the new ideas—at least new to mainstream Westerners—that have been creeping up on us in recent decades, such as transcendental meditation, yoga, and various types of energy healing. She found that by following some of these spiritual disciplines she began to get quieter inside.

"All of the noise that we have in our heads," Nedda said, "is a distraction that keeps us from hearing telepathic information come in. So one of the first things we need to learn is how to be quiet—really, really quiet.

"People say to me, you talk to the animals. I say, Yes, I do, but more important, *I listen*. That's the critical thing, being able to hear. And of course I use that word loosely, because we get pictures and emotions, it's not necessarily sound. But basically, the first step is to be psychologically open to the fact that animals are full, intelligent beings. They are as full beings as you or I. I'm talking about horses, cats, insects, the wind, and the plants. The earth is a gene, it is alive. Everything in the universe is composed of energy, and God is the fabric from which the universe is made."

ROSE IS ROSE by Pat Brady

ROSE IS ROSE reprinted by permission of United Feature Syndicate, Inc.

5

The Complicated Emotional Lives of Animals

People try to communicate with animals for a variety of reasons. Many simply want a closer, more sociable, and more loving relationship with their pets. Others are seeking a better understanding of the mystical interrelation between the disparate—yet not so disparate—beings of our universe.

When these beings are animals, the purpose is often therapy. Professional animal communicators are usually called in when something seems to ail the animal, something that appears to be beyond the ken of conventional veterinarians. Many—in fact, most—animal communicators work closely with vets.

An animal's problem can be physical or psychological, and I plan to provide illustrations of both kinds throughout this book. In this chapter, I will relate accounts from communicators, clients, and witnesses that involve the emotional lives of animals.

Phil Roberts, who lives near Camden, Maine, specializes in the psychological problems of animals, which sometimes involve behavioral difficulties.

"If you have an animal with a problem," he said, "if it bites, pees on the floor, if you have a horse who doesn't like being shod, then I can talk to them and perhaps find out the reasons and help them."

Like many professional animal communicators, Phil shies away from the physical problems of animals. "Legally," he says, "working with physical ailments can become a problem. But I have very good relations with the veterinarians around here. They send people to me—people whose animals seem to be having emotional troubles—and I send people to them, people whose animals are having physical illnesses."

At one time Phil and his wife, Dinny Thorndike, owned a dairy farm in New Hampshire. They eventually sold the place and moved to the coast of Maine.

"I've always been close to animals," Phil told me. "The reason we stopped having cows is that when a cow can't work there's nothing to do but kill it, ship it for meat. And that bothered me so much we stopped doing it. We had to leave the farm because there were too many horrible associations with the place. I would have nightmares about cows dying."

Phil settled down in Maine and worked with Dinny at producing books, a harmless occupation for the most part. She does the writing, he helps with interviewing and research. At times, the couple boarded a horse belonging to Patty Breed, who spends part of the year in Florida and part in Maine. I met Patty and Dinny at Patty's Florida home. Patty figures prominently later in this book for her contacts with undomesticated animals, as well as other aspects of nature—chairs, for example. Yes, chairs. They have wood, don't they? Patty was an unusual child— and is an unusual adult, for that matter. She had become involved in animal communication, and passed her interest on to Phil and Dinny, who took a trip to California for a workshop with Jeri Ryan, a well-known teacher in the field.

According to Phil, the day he got back from that workshop people started asking him to talk with their animals.

"Everybody can do this," Phil says, "we're all born with the ability. I think I learned quickly because I've been close to animals. Also, I've studied self-hypnosis. Hypnosis came very easy to me. It's easy for me to concentrate, let go, and call up the animals."

"One thing that was recommended in the workshop we took was to ask something to prove to people that we really talked with the animal. I try to do that. Early on, I asked a dog if there was anything important he wanted to tell me. Nothing came through except for the color green. It was important to the dog. It didn't make any sense to me right off, so I asked the owner if there was something in her house that was important to the dog and that was green. She gave it some thought and then mentioned that she had a green bedspread that the dog was not supposed to lie on. But he very much liked to lie on that bedspread, and he would do it when she wasn't around.

"Then there was this pony. Something was bothering him, and I thought it might be a rat. The pony told me that it had large ears and it was white. The pony also said he preferred to eat out of a green bucket. When I talked this over with the owner, it developed that there was a Jack Russell terrier who would bother the pony and steal its grain. If the owner put the grain in this green bucket it was better for the horse because that bucket had higher sides and the terrier couldn't get at the grain."

At the time I talked with Phil, he was about two-thirds of the way through the cats at the Camden-Rockport Animal Rescue League. "It's my latest project," he told me. "The league is a local animal shelter. They have 106 cats. I've been talking to two of them every night. It's fascinating. The league keeps the cats. Many are not suitable for adoption. Some are quite old. With some of them, their owners died and left sums to the league, and the league keeps the cat happy the rest of its life."

Phil conducts this project from his home—telepathically. "Distance means absolutely nothing," he says. "I talk to California and other distant places." He has visited the league's quarters physically only once, to see a dog that seemed extraordinarily like a dog he had once owned that had died. "I had a suspicion that it might be my dog and that he had come back," Phil relates, "so I had to go and talk to him. It wasn't the same dog, but it was a very, very similar dog."

Every morning, two women staff members at the shelter pick out two cats they want Phil to work with that night. "I give them the results of the previous night and they give me two more. All I need to know is the name, the breed, the sex, if it's been neutered, the color. Generally, that's enough.

Phil Roberts and Foxy; photo by Virginia Thorndike

"I introduce myself to the animal. I say, 'They asked me to talk with you. Is there anything you'd like to say? Is there anything I can help you with? They told me you are very shy. Is there something that's bothering you?' A lot of times I want to know the animal's history. One thing the animals never do is say anything bad. Even in extremely abusive cases it's very hard for them to say anything negative. I don't find them angry."

During my extensive interviewing of animal communicators, I did not find this always to be the case. Some animals—particularly those in zoos—were plenty angry, my interviewees reported. Of course, the cats that Phil Roberts was chatting with at the league were housed in a very benign atmosphere.

A talk with one particular cat stands out in Phil's memory:

When I visited the place, there was a really striking gray cat, with brilliant markings and wonderful eyes. The next time the girls called me they asked me to come to him. His name was Boy. He was seventeen. His owner had died and left him to the shelter. He's starting to fail. But he's comfortable, not in any pain, and he liked watching all the activity. They sometimes have kittens who are born there, and he really liked that, watching the kittens grow up. He said I could ask him *anything*.

The previous cat I had done there, named Marty, had had a problem with biting. Marty had been declawed, a horrendous thing to do to a cat. Cats that don't have claws tend to bite. I asked Boy if Marty would stop biting. He replied, "No, no, no, ask me *important* things. Ask me if the snow will melt, ask me about rainbows, about sunsets."

The next morning, when I called in to report my talk with Boy, I was told that he was having a stroke. He came out of it, and he's all right. But animals know about these things, they know what's going on in their bodies, what's going to happen. So Boy wanted to talk about important stuff. He wanted to say that whether he gets old, has a stroke, and dies, the world is going to go on, there will be sunsets. They have *incredibly* wonderful lessons to teach us!

As I was writing this account of Boy, I was reminded of an anecdote I heard some twenty-five years ago from friends in Lenox, Massachusetts, about a cat named Michael. At twenty-one, Michael was an oldie but very much a goodie, still perking along famously. Also, it would appear that he was quite psychic—maybe even for a cat.

Michael was the pet of a family named Librizzi, whom I knew well. Joel Librizzi was a photographer who often did work for a regional magazine of which I was the editor. Tara, his wife, was a professor of psychology and philosophy at two state colleges in Berkshire County, at the far western edge of Massachusetts. They had two children, a boy named Marc and a girl, like her mother, named Tara. Marc, who was fourteen at the time of this incident, is now a professor of English at the University of Maine. Tara was thirteen and is now an actress and social worker. The elder Tara has recently retired as a professor of philosophy at the University of Maine.

It might be pertinent to mention that the elder Tara is very psychic, very much into doing Tarot cards, giving psychic readings, and seeing ghosts. And to some extent, so were the kids. It was a family where Michael really belonged. I can recall one day seeing him gazing intently out the window. I wondered aloud what he was looking at. Tara commented that it probably was something we couldn't see.

One day Michael did something uncharacteristic: he got sick. The Librizzis took him to a vet in Stockbridge, six miles away. The vet told them they would have to leave Michael overnight. That evening, the family went to a movie. When they got home, they waited on the porch while the elder Tara fished in her purse for the house keys. Suddenly they saw Michael come running around the side of the house, leap up on the porch, and go to the front door. This was something he often did. Tara automatically opened the door, and Michael ran in. His nightly custom was to run to the kitchen and grab a snack from his dish.

But it was "Wait a minute!" time for the Librizzis. Hadn't they taken Michael to the vet that afternoon? They ran in, and Michael was nowhere to be seen. They called the vet's. They were told that Michael was still crouched morosely in the cage he had been put in that afternoon. What had happened?

The assumption is that Michael had been yearning so much to be back among his accustomed surroundings that he had taken an astral trip home. When the Librizzis appeared on the porch, Michael was able to materialize for a moment, and they saw him.

You must admit it's a fun story, and when I recently spoke with the Librizzis while writing this they all gave exactly the same accounts as they had years ago. This always impresses an interviewer. I recall a great line that Tara gave me about Michael. She told me that in their adolescence her kids had been worried about Michael. They had known him all their lives, and at such an advanced age, they reasoned, he couldn't last much longer on this earthly plane.

"But I told them," Tara said, "don't worry, that cat's not going anywhere."

Animals are obviously not immune from many of the disquieting emotional situations that human flesh is heir to. Sexual discrimination, for example. Betty Lewis of Amherst, New Hampshire, comes up with an intriguing story about a female Great Dane who was suffering an acute case of sexual discrimination. The story isn't as cosmic as that of Boy, Phil Roberts's deep-thinking kitty, or even Michael's six-mile astral trip, but it really shook this Great Dane. When Betty told me the story she repeatedly referred to the dog as a bitch. The term sort of shook me. It didn't seem a polite way to speak of this unhappy and completely inoffensive lady dog. But I guess that's the way dedicated dog people talk.

Here is the story that Betty, who is a Great Dane breeder, told me:

I guess this is my crowning glory in the Great Dane world. I'm not sure if dog show people are harder to convince about animal communication than other people are, but being accepted in that group is difficult. So I was very surprised when a professional handler came to me and said she had a client who owned this Great Dane bitch. They thought she had the potential to become the number one Great Dane that year. But the dog had suddenly stopped making an effort in her shows, and without her cooperation there wasn't going to be any winning. They wanted me to talk with her and see what the problem was. So I did, and she said, "It's because I'm a girl."

At first I didn't understand what she meant. Then a friend told me that the lady who owned the dog valued her male dogs more than her female dogs. Therefore this bitch felt she wasn't as worthy as a male, and that she was going to be stopped from showing after she finished her championship. And also, the character of the showings had changed because the owner and the handler had become very focused on the winning rather than just breezing through and having a good time. The dog became intimidated by their intensity. The focus on winning changed the dog's enjoyment of what they were doing. It changed all of their enjoyment. The dog also felt that if she didn't try she couldn't fail.

So I talked with the woman, and she agreed to write down the reasons that she thought this dog was worth putting money into. This would focus the value of the dog in her mind. And she also promised that after the dog finished campaigning for the year she would be able to have a litter of puppies, which was something that the dog had told me that she wanted.

I spoke with the dog on a Saturday, telling her all this, and on Sunday in the show ring she was totally a different dog. She went on to become the number one Great Dane in the nation in 1993. She was the first black and the first female to attain number one. And she did have her litter of puppies.

Animals have as many hang-ups as we humans, it would seem. And their plights are not all that different from ours. Witness the psychotherapy that Nedda Wittels got involved in while working with a Doberman.

"This lady came to me," Nedda relates, "because she was having a problem with a Doberman named Shadow. The dog was very shy. In fact, it acted as though it was scared of its shadow."

Nedda talked with Shadow telepathically for about an hour. "For some reason," she told me, "I kept wanting to call the dog Thunder. Finally, I got the woman on the line and asked her, 'Who is Thunder?' And an interesting tale developed. The woman said that when she was looking for a dog she had planned to get a powerful dog."

But as it turned out the woman hadn't found such a dog. She got instead a dog who was delicate and elegant. She had picked out the name Thunder in advance, but that was inappropriate for this dog, so she called him Shadow.

Nedda said, "At this point, the dog is practically shouting at me, 'I want to be called Thunder!' He said he could be brave and strong if he was called Thunder.

"It would be wonderful if I could say that with his name change his whole personality changed. But in fact, although the woman started calling the dog Thunder, deep inside her she still thought of him as Shadow. She wrote me a note saying she was calling the dog Thunder but he hadn't reacted as though he were any more aggressive or braver. I told her that personality does not change overnight. And *she* hadn't made the psychological transition either. In her letter, sometimes she called the dog Thunder and sometimes Shadow."

And you, dear reader, think *human* relationships are complicated! The poor dog knew he was still Shadow to this woman. You can't fool an animal. They're reading us like a book.

"I believe," Nedda says, "that when we go to pick out an animal they are reading us. It's amazing how they understand everything. When we talk about them in front of them as though they are pieces of furniture, it is just as rude as if we were talking in front of a child as though the child didn't exist."

This next anecdote concerns a dog named Jessie, also known as Cookie Butt, who was a bibliophobe. I think I made up that word, it's not in my 2,140-page dictionary. I figure it means the opposite of bibliophile, which *is* in the dictionary, and which means "lover of books." Cookie Butt—or Jessie—hated books. She used to tear them apart, along with any papers that happened to be lying around.

Jessie belonged to Celeste Bowman of Katy, Texas. When Jessie was six, she was acquired by Celeste, and her life took a sharp turn for the better. Jessie had been kicked by her former owner, hit in the head with a beer bottle, and abandoned when the man moved. She sat for days in front of the house, waiting for him to return. Finally she went wandering, looking for food, and eventually found a home with Celeste. Happy ending? Should be, so why was Cookie Butt tearing up Celeste's books and papers when Celeste was at work? Celeste brought in Griffin Kanter, a well-known animal communicator from nearby Houston. Griffin had some talks with Jessie.

"Sometimes abused animals wait until they are in a safer environment, and then they act out," Griffin told me. "They still have all that anger."

Jessie had become very dependent on Celeste, and when Celeste would leave the house Jessie would have, as Celeste put it, "terrible separation anxiety."

"She was angry," Celeste said, "because when I was home I was surrounded at my desk with books and papers, and she felt I was ignoring her. She would get upset when she was left alone during the day when I was at work, and books and papers were the natural thing for her to go for. She felt they were causing the separation."

Celeste attended one of Griffin's workshops and became adept at communication. Together, Griffin and Celeste worked with Jessie. Griffin used some interesting psychotherapy to get at the dog's problem.

"We talked with the dog in Jessie who tried to please humans but couldn't avoid being abused," Griffin said. "Then we talked with the killer dog in Jessie, who wanted to go for everybody's throat. We put that negative energy of Jessie's on a figurative leash and took her outside, and Celeste would talk with her about how she herself had been in situations of abuse as a child, and how she had worked with that anger. It helped Jessie to see that she wasn't the only one it had happened to, and that Celeste was willing to work with her."

It's now eight years later, and Jessie is a happy dog. She and Celeste have great communication.

Nancy Regalmuto is a clairvoyant whom I have known to perform extraordinary feats of mysticism. She is based in New York City and adjacent Long Island. She is possibly the leading animal communicator working with horses, but she works with other animals too. The following story is a bit mundane—a pet pooch who insisted on urinating in inconvenient places—compared with some of Nancy's achievements, but it's indicative of her insight and ingenuity. Nancy told me:

He was a small terrier in a large home on the water in Port Jefferson. He was about eight, and for eight years they had had trainers trying to deal with his problem. And that was that he peed all over the house. He never defecated, only peed. The trainers would say, "Lady, your dog is nuts." So she decided to take him to a nut doctor, i.e., me.

When I started to talk to him, I realized why everyone thought he was nuts. He was not what you would call a typically balanced animal. They had tried a variety of things, such as putting his nose into the pee or giving him a little spanking. Or they would put him in a big crate when they'd go out. The trouble was, he didn't understand this at all, he didn't see it as a punishment, he felt the crate was his home.

The dog told me he had a fascination with cleaning. When I told this to the woman, she said, "That's absolutely right, when I clean house, he follows me all around."

The dog was under the impression that the floor was his domain, because he was so close to the floor. He felt that the floor was his responsibility, that it was his job to keep the floor clean. He was resentful of anything that was used to clean the floor—such as the vacuum cleaner, which he would bark at. He felt the same way about the outside property, too; he'd get upset with the lawn mower and the rake.

He was like some people, in that he had a cleaning fetish. He'd watch the woman spray cleaning fluid, like Glass Plus®, and then she'd wipe where she'd sprayed. He saw how the spray came out of the container. He'd look at his own spray, and how it came out of him. When the woman would clean up his urine, she'd wipe it just as she had wiped up the cleaning fluid. He didn't quite get the difference. He felt he had cleaning fluid inside of him. He felt he was doing her a favor. He took great pride in cleaning. He could not comprehend that he was being punished for doing this.

So I sprayed some Glass Plus® on the floor, near where he had put some of his urine. I had him smell both. He was a bit dense. I wondered how I was going to get this through to him. He'd been doing this for years, and he really felt he was providing a service. I didn't want to take away his pride, or his natural desire to want to help. So I projected to him that his urine was offensive to us. Not that *he* was offensive, but the urine was. It caused a problem in our noses. I visualized myself having trouble breathing. I visualized his mistress cleaning up his urine, being upset. I sent that vibration. I visualized her getting down and wiping it up, the vibration of her breathing and being upset. We were communicating through mental telepathy. There are vibrations to someone being angry and there are vibrations to someone being happy. I visualized her emotional energy. He could feel the tension I was projecting. I was seeing her on her knees, coughing.

I let him know that she loved him. I made a picture of her holding him, loving him. I sent love vibrations, but simultaneously sent the picture of her on her knees on the floor, very unhappy with him. And I'm saying verbally to him in my mind, "She doesn't like this." Then I visualized a scene of him when he had to urinate, going to the back door, her letting him out, and him going to a tree and urinating. Raising his leg, the urine coming out. His smelling the urine on the ground, coming back into the house and her greeting him with love.

SYLVIA by Nicole Hollander

© 1996 by Nicole Hollander.

I said, "We all know that you like to help." I showed him how to empty garbage into a wastebasket, like a piece of paper on the floor and putting it into the wastebasket. How to pick up shoes and put them in a closet, different tasks. I gave him other outlets on how to help. I visualized it and verbalized it—silent verbalizing; I never spoke out loud.

This dog was motivated by love. Love and service was his motivation, and that's what I used. He would not have responded to food. There was a cat in the house, but he would not have responded through competitiveness or jealousy. That would not have worked. What this little dog wanted was acceptance and approval. He was just slightly mixed up on how to get it.

"The animals are here to teach us," Nancy told me. "A lot of people find it easier to get close to an animal than to other people. It's not as threatening. If you speak to people who get very close to animals, you hear things like, 'I'd marry my dog if he were a man.' You'll find out that often in their childhood they were turned off on mankind. They may have suffered some kind of abuse. Or they may have had some kind of physical or emotional problem that wasn't adequately understood and the only place they felt comfortable was with animals. So a lot of people actually have their animals as their psychiatrists."

The relationship is not always healthful for the animal. This is an example that Nancy told me about:

I was called in to do a reading on a horse, and the horse said, "I know you're here to do a reading on me, but she [the horse's young owner] needs more help than I do. She's in trouble, she's a drug addict, and she's in a lot of pain. She's tried to kill herself a number of times. Her family doesn't pay any attention to her."

The horse went into a description about the girl. This happens to me many times. I end up reading not only the animal but the person. Sometimes the animal will tell me, but sometimes I'm concentrating on the relationship and the person comes into play, their problems are creating a dynamic between them and their animal. I have to read both and say, "If you want your animal to be healed you need to heal, you need to do this and that."

One horse I saw was dying, and nobody could find out why. He had hardly any flesh on him, he was depressed, no luster to his coat. A teenage girl had called me in. The horse was dying because this girl was being abused by her parents. They would beat her unmercifully. She would come to the barn, the only place where she felt comfort, and while she was upset and disturbed she would get on her horse and would exchange energy with her horse. Animals are very compassionate, and they will take on your pain. All of that misery and pain she would give to him. After she got off him she would feel a great deal better, but he'd feel so much worse. He had gotten to the point where he couldn't handle her pain anymore, and it was affecting him on a physical level.

So I told her how to deal with her pain before she got on the horse. I told her she had great skills as a poet. She needed to go someplace and write poetry, and heal after bad things happened at home. That she needed to get these feelings out before she got with her animal because there was an energy exchange happening that was very unhealthy for the animal. I taught her how to be by herself, how to channel her creative energies in a positive and constructive way. Her animal was there as a friend, not to take on her negativity. It's one thing to communicate with a friend, it's another thing to give him all your negative energy.

———

Donetta Zimmerman of Cincinnati is a personnel officer in a corporation. In her spare time, she communicates with animals. She does it as a hobby, preferring not to charge for her services. She told me, "I feel that if I said, I need X amount of dollars to see your animal, that I would feel that I was obligated to perform, and there are times when I am not getting good information."

Despite her modesty, Donetta has an excellent batting average, and is well regarded throughout the Midwest. A communication that stands out in her memory involves a horse named Rags. It illustrates a frequent aspect of animal communication, which is that some owners can be afraid to find out what the animal says—they are worried that the animal may be unhappy, or worse, that the animal may not like them.

"This horse was by far the most intelligent animal I've ever talked to," Donetta told me. He was a dressage horse in the Vandalia-Troy, Ohio, area. I had talked to many horses in the barn, and several had mentioned this horse. They would refer to him as the horse everybody watches. Many were jealous of him, some wanted to be like him, but they all conveyed that this light-colored horse got all the attention. Everyone talked to him and about him.

"I asked the owners where this horse was. They said they didn't want me to talk with him. They were afraid he was unhappy, and they didn't want to know that. But I insisted, and I did talk to the horse. And he was very happy. The people were delighted to hear that."

Donetta Zimmerman

I asked Donetta what seemed so intelligent about this horse, and she replied:

He understood what I was doing. He communicated with many people beautifully. He talked about his trainer, with whom he communicated very well. He talked about a former rider who communicated mentally with him very well. He told me, "I can do well with anyone if they just sit back and hold on and let me do the work. Then I can perform beautifully. I practice best when I'm by myself." And he showed me himself in a field going through his paces.

The trainer said, "That's exactly what he does. When we send him out in the field at night to give him a little pasture time, he goes through his paces all by himself out there."

They thought it was hysterical, they thought it was funny. That's when he thought he was getting the best training, when he was out there practicing all by himself. He was like a human athlete who would be out running the track over and over late at night.

———

Diana Thompson is a well-known horse trainer based in Santa Rosa, California. A few years ago, while she was rehabilitating a horse who had been demoralized and physically damaged in the world of racing, she approached Penelope Smith, perhaps the best known of animal communicators. She did this with considerable skepticism. As Diana put it to me, "I thought it was a bunch of baloney, but why not try it. The horse was still in a lot of trouble and was dreadfully emotional."

In the course of one phone call, Penelope convinced this highly experienced and practical horsewoman that telepathy and other mystical aspects of animal communication were no baloney. Diana has incorporated these precepts into her own work, and has passed them on to others. One of these others is Stacy Winter.

Stacy teaches second grade in Moorpark, about forty-five miles north of Los Angeles. She is very active in dressage. This is her story and that of her horse Major Henry:

I had an extraordinary experience with Diana Thompson that has completely impacted the way I deal with all animals. What Diana did was make sense of things that we question in life. We don't know if they are coincidental or if it's our subconscious, or whatever. And now I understand that it's communication. When you find that you are sensitive to that communication, it opens up a whole new world.

I went to a ranch where they buy horses and oxen and ship them for slaughter. I went there to pick up a specific horse, but I had to go back to the truck because I was so overcome with emotion at the sight of all these horses so desperately looking for their owners. They were looking for a familiar face, a person who was going to get them out of a terribly, terribly humiliating situation, which those slaughter pens are.

Many of these horses are clipped for show; they're family horses, they're beautiful. You also have the other end of the scale—some are ill or seriously lame. All of these horses were to be shipped for slaughter. There were about 180 horses there.

One horse lifted his head and walked toward the front of the pen, as though he recognized me. I knew I had to leave that property with that horse. He was a stallion, twelve years old. He was Kentucky bred, with a very famous sire, Verbatim. His name was Major Henry. He had been purchased as a track horse, then had an accident. Then he was purchased by a man here in California, as a stud. He was with that man for seven years. I was trying to figure out how such a beautiful animal, a stallion no less, had ended up in this absolutely pathetic situation of a slaughter pen.

I looked at his papers, and he seemed to be in excellent condition. I bought him, but couldn't take him that day. When I went back, three days later, I couldn't even recognize him. He had lost about 120 pounds in that short period. He looked like his spirit had been broken, as though any confidence and self-esteem he had had been shattered. He looked lifeless. We got him out of that killing pen and loaded him onto the trailer.

I wondered if I had made a great mistake. This horse was twelve years old, he hadn't been under saddle for eight years. And I wanted to train him as a dressage horse, which is a highly technical form of riding. Everything was working against me, except my intuition. I knew I had to have this horse. It wasn't clear to me why, but I had to get that horse out of that environment.

For three months, the horse did everything in its power to kill me. He was angry, bitter, frightened, disoriented. He constantly looked as though he was searching for somebody. He always looked over my head, beyond me.

I was with him hour after hour, because I was trying to crack through his hard shell, and he would have nothing to do with me. But I was never frightened, I hung in there. Everybody told me he was a killer, I should take him back.

I went to a new trainer, who had entirely new ways of approaching a horse, from homeopathy to chiropractic. She was a New Age trainer. From her I learned about Diana Thompson and her type of hands-on horse care. I had never been involved in anything like this. I thought I knew everything about horses—I'd been involved with them for twenty-five years. I thought I had nothing to learn from the new stuff that was coming in. Little did I know it was going to change my life.

I went to a hands-on clinic given by Diana. I quickly realized she was empowering me to save horses' and animals' lives if they were frightened or traumatized.

Throughout the clinic, it had been clear to me that Diana had the ability to communicate with animals. That wasn't part of the package; it wasn't disclosed that she did that. But it was clear to me that she was getting pictures or some kind of communication from these horses that permitted her to deal with each horse very specifically and individually, and deal with the owner. I felt this had to come from each horse. She could pinpoint specific instances in the horse's experience that affected its behavior. The owners would confirm these things, that they had happened. It was uncanny. It was spooky to me.

She walked up to Major's stall and turned to her assistant, Adrian Moore, a veterinarian who was working with her on this particular clinic. They gave each other a look. Diana said to me that this horse is not ready to be worked on, he needs time to himself for a little while. I wrapped him and took him out. About two hours later, she walked into his stall. He was really agitated. I wondered what she was getting. She had come into this without any knowledge of the horse whatever. Diana asked her assistant if she was picking up the same thing, and Adrian said yes. Diana turned to me and said, "Who's Bill?"

I was astounded. Because Bill was Major's previous owner. His name was Bill Elrod. He had died. He and Major had had this very strong, very loving relationship. Major was the pride and joy of this man's life. In Bill's presence, Major felt very important, very valuable and regal.

When Bill had died, his wife asked a neighbor down the road to board Major at her stable. This neighbor had thrown hay to Major for eight months. He was not handled, turned out, he was not dealt with in any way. He received no affection. He was cut off from his former loving relationship and did not understand where Bill was. The neighbor finally said she could no longer board Major, and Bill's wife said to sell him. The neighbor quite innocently took the horse to an auction, hoping to sell him to a good owner, but he was bought up by the brokers, the killer buyers.

When I explained to Diana who Bill was, she turned to Major and explained to him that Bill had died. The horse was very agitated. Diana explained that Bill was not going to come back. But she sent pictures that Bill was indeed Major's guardian angel, because he had sent me to Major. It made complete sense to me, because I couldn't understand why I had bought that horse, who was in no way compatible with my interests as a horse owner.

When Diana told him all this, Major gave a deep shudder. His body drooped, and he went back into the stall. He had tears in his eyes, which is very unusual for a horse. For the first time, he licked my hand and accepted me. My relationship with this horse has become the most intense and accepting. Not only with this horse, but with animals in general.

I think I have always had an ability to communicate with animals to a certain degree, but I didn't understand it. Now I understand it. I communicate with animals through pictures. I can do it from far away. It comes from the silence. I would never have found the puzzle piece if I had not known Diana. This has changed my life.

6

How Communicators Have Helped Heal Animals Physically

egally speaking, the physical healing of animals by people who are not licensed veterinarians can be a risky business. It's a minefield onto which many animal communicators are reluctant to tread. Many veterinarians admire communicators; they seek or at least accept their assistance. But there are also many close-minded vets, as well as vets who feel threatened by competition for their services, for their status, not to mention clients' dollars. A number of communicators have been targets of legal action by veterinary associations. Later in this chapter we'll hear from an extraordinarily knowledgeable veterinarian who is equipped to discuss both sides of the equation.

But first I would like to convey why I am certain that healing can be accomplished psychically. For several years, I knew an extraordinary healer. I wrote articles about him in magazines, and included a chapter on his early life in a children's book—*Kids Do Amazing Things*. His name was Sam Lentine.

Sam was not only a psychic, he was also a scientist. He held a doctorate in biophysics. When I first knew him he was teaching physics at Rensselaer Polytechnic Institute in Troy, New York. He was blind. He had lost his eyes to cancer at the age of one. He eventually died of brain cancer at forty-eight. In between, he lived a life of accomplishment and ebullience. In school, he was a wrestler and a judo expert. He led a prize-winning jazz band. He was a star debater. As an adult, he was a founder of a national organization called the United States Psychotronics Association, which brought together physicists, chemists, and psychics. Since Sam was all three, he was something of a one-man bridge to the twenty-first century.

Sam was aware as a child of his psychic abilities, and as a young man he worked toward developing his diagnostic and healing talents. Like many animal communicators, he could see into the body. He wanted to diagnose and to heal. He began working with physicians and studying anatomy and physiology. And soon he began to suffer the problems that come with being ahead of one's time. His unorthodox talents crippled his academic career. He ran headlong into the ortho-doxy, the fear of the unknown that has always obstructed the advance-ment of science. He turned from college teaching to working with doctors and research laboratories.

In the first article I wrote on Sam, in 1983, I interviewed several doctors he had worked with. One, a Dr. Thomas Couch of Albany, New York, said, among other things, "I've worked with Sam on well over a dozen cases. They were potentially explosive situations and his diag-noses were astoundingly accurate. Sam picked up several situations where there was danger of ruptures, and these were successfully treated by surgery."

I interviewed a number of people who had been healed by Sam. One was a woman named Achsa Meager, of Dilltown, Pennsylvania. Sam did most of his healing at a distance, telepathically, but in this case Achsa traveled to his home in Troy. She told me:

I came to Sam's house in such pain that I couldn't stand it any longer. It was in the lower part of my back. My son had to help me into the house. When I came out, it dawned on me all of a sudden that I had no pain. I haven't had any since. I had been doctoring for a long time. I went to specialists but got no relief. I had a back operation in 1960. The incision, which was perfectly straight up and down, went crooked. The pain started and I couldn't put my right leg down straight. The specialist said there was nothing he could do; he left me no hope.

This is what Sam told me about the case:

There were problems with disks. It looked like there was a lot of degeneration going on. I never make promises to people when I'm working on them. I can't because I just don't know what's going to happen. Achsa was one in whom I felt immediate results. I don't know how it happened, it just did. I could feel her receptivity and her good response. Probably what I did helped to reduce the inflammation and caused the disks to reverse their degeneration. It's a healing process. I become a channel and allow the healing energies to come in and do the work.

I could give many examples of Sam's successes in healing—a woman he cured of phlebitis in one afternoon; a boy he helped cure of severe headaches by diagnosing an aneurysm; a nurse in Virginia who had had an inoperable brain tumor for years, which disappeared within hours after Sam and his group worked on her case long distance. I spoke with each of these women and the boy's mother, as well as other patients, physicians, and witnesses. Sam also taught diagnosis and healing, and his groups had many successes. He had a core group that I occasionally attended, although as far as I know I never developed any abilities of this sort.

I noticed that on his professional card Sam identified himself as a diagnostician, not as a healer. It's pretty obvious why. While researching this book, I spoke with Anita Curtis, an animal communicator in Gilbertsville, Pennsylvania. When I told her about Sam's card, she said, "I don't blame him—the AMA, they'll go right for your throat." Anita takes no chances in her practice, which she confines to animals, although she admits that she seems to have cured her husband of an abdominal aortic aneurysm. But she plays it very cool in her professional activities.

"I won't even learn anatomy," she told me. "I don't know the names of the muscles, the bones, the vertebrae, anything. I'll tell the person, run your hand along the shoulder and come down about an inch, that's where it hurts on the horse. I won't get into naming, or anything like that. I feel that if something like that is going on they should go to the vet. I leave it up to the medical field. I also recommend certain vets who I know are excellent and who will listen to what I have to say."

Anita belongs to the cautious wing of the communicators fraternity—
or should we call it sorority, since an overwhelming majority of communicators are women? But Kate Reilly of Shelby, North Carolina, one
of the country's leading practitioners of the art, belongs to the other
pole—the let-it-all-hang-out, let-the-chips-fall-where-they-may school of
animal communication. When she first got into the field, she told me,
she was warned by senior communicators not to diagnose things. "But
my attitude," she said, "is that I am the advocate of the animals, and if
I don't help them . . ."

Kate is a reporter's delight. She doesn't hold back. She tells it as she
sees it. Here's what she told me:

> The healing aspect, I've been doing my whole life. I could always go
> inside people's bodies and feel what they felt and tell them what their
> physical problems were. My background is in health and physical edu-
> cation, so I know anatomy and physiology. I taught health and phys-
> ical education for a short time after graduating from college, but my
> basic job was training racehorses and I did that for twenty years. I
> discovered there was more there than people thought, that there was
> an intelligent being that I could relate to differently from other peo-
> ple. When I heard about Penelope Smith, I was incredibly interested
> because I felt that it was valid. I took a workshop with her, as well as
> with Jeri Ryan.
>
> As a child, I knew I could bring down swelling and drop tempera-
> tures, that sort of thing. Nothing monumental, just little things. I
> thought everyone could do that. And when I found out they couldn't,
> I sort of hid it. After I had children of my own, I would use those abil-
> ities with them, and also with the horses I was training. I didn't do ani-
> mal communication publicly until my children grew up and left home.
> I didn't want to do anything that would make my kids look weird.
>
> But later I began to get into it. For example, I worked on a horse
> and told his owner that his vertebrae were out of alignment, which
> ones they were, and how they were turned. The horse had a really
> sore back. His owner took him to [a famous veterinary school] and
> had him x-rayed, and my diagnosis was exactly correct. As a result,
> the school used me for a couple of things. The same is true of [another
> well-known veterinarian center]. It's a very concrete proof of what you

do, as opposed to purely emotional questions like: Is my horse happy and does he like where he lives?

And yet if you speak with [the first school] they'll tell you that animal communication is a hoax. Because it takes away from what they do. And yet there are people there who will privately acknowledge what I do. A couple of times, the head of surgery at [the second place mentioned above] got on the phone with me. But they won't acknowledge such things. And then they do interviews in publications that deal with animals and say animal communication is a joke.

———————

I'd like to interject something here. They say there are no coincidences, which may be true, who knows? Anyway, as I was typing the above paragraph I decided to break for lunch. I picked up a book I had been reading, *Channeling*, by Jon Klimo, and opened it. These words greeted my eyes:

> In his recent book, *Deviant Science: The Case of Parapsychology*, University of Pennsylvania professor James McClenon speaks of the problems in our culture of being considered deviant for pursuing anomalies (such as channeling) that have what he calls "low ontological status." This means that such phenomena are seen as having relatively low reality compared to our usual experience of what is real. "Deviance," [McClenon] writes, "can be defined as 'those acts, attributes, and beliefs which, when performed or made known . . . elicit an evaluative social sanction.'" That is, by their beliefs and actions, the deviant court is being put back in line with the larger social structure and belief system. The scientist who stays open to the possible reality of channeling runs into this problem by holding what McClenon calls "beliefs . . . that violate some of the [current] metaphysical foundations of science."

I'll grant that this is written in classic academese. But murky though it is, I feel it says a mouthful. In English, I would say it means that many people—especially highly educated, highly trained people— have to be dragged kicking and screaming into the presence of any idea that they weren't given permission to believe during the course of their hard-won education. For example, ideas such as communicating with animals or healing through means that are not taught in conventional medical schools. The traditionally accepted beliefs and practices have provided their practitioners with such generous rewards in prestige and finances that to question them could be troubling, both objectively and subjectively.

But let's get back to the adventures of Kate Reilly. She told me:

A woman called me about a thoroughbred mare that sometimes lost the ability to function muscularly. The horse was falling down all the time. This was a last-ditch effort on her owner's part because several veterinarians had advised her to put the horse down. The last group of vets were from [another famous veterinarian college]. They had tested her extensively and wanted her donated so they could study her and then put her down.

When I talked with the horse, she said she didn't know what they were talking about. She was sure she didn't have any kind of disease. She said she had been a jumper and had crashed over one of the jumps and landed on her back and that her back was out of alignment, and it was causing her to lose the feeling in her front legs. Because she couldn't feel her front legs, she would occasionally trip over them and fall down. When I checked her body and found where the vertebrae had been turned I felt that this was true, and suggested that the woman contact a chiropractor and acupuncturist, and told her where the vertebrae were. And the horse recovered so totally that the college did another evaluation, and said something's wrong here. The mare went on to do third-level dressage and her owner bred her after that. She's not a brand-new horse, but she doesn't fall down anymore and doesn't have the loss of muscle control. Because they couldn't see inside her body and couldn't feel what I was feeling, they couldn't diagnose it correctly.

I train veterinarians to do this, that's a large part of what I do. Last weekend, I had a workshop at which there were three veterinarians attending. They were there because over and over their clients had said, "My psychic says . . . " and it was correct. The vets became interested because of the accuracy. I've had many physicians in my classes—emergency room physicians, pediatric physicians, orthopedic physicians, all kinds of medical personnel.

Kate Reilly snuggles a friend

I told Kate that in my interviews with communicators I was constantly—almost invariably—getting the message that *anyone* can communicate with animals. But, I asked, is the talent for *healing* so common? She replied:

There aren't that many who can do healing. But I think everyone has the ability to do certain things beyond what they know they can. For instance, move energy, which can cause healing in some cases. They can make changes in the physical bodies of animals, or people, or whatever. But unless they are aware of it, they never do it, so consequently it doesn't exist, you know. Of all the people I teach in workshops—hundreds and hundreds and hundreds—there were very few who can go inside a body and pinpoint the things that are not correct, and draw conclusions. A lot of it is fear, I think. For instance, veterinarians may know that an animal is in pain, but they don't want to experience that pain, even in a lesser degree, which is what we get. So they're on the outside of a body, looking in, they're not actually inside.

Let me say one thing about this whole area: people are very hesitant to discuss it. Even humans I've worked on. Like a burn victim whose burn went away. Or a person who was attacked by wasps, and the result of the stings went away. They will not discuss it. There are people I've known almost my whole life who will come to me for help but will never tell anyone else. So when you ask for people who I have worked on or with, there are some whose names I can give you, but the overall majority will not want to discuss it. And that includes veterinarians, very much so.

One of Kate Reilly's most ardent admirers is Dr. Dave Jefferson, a graduate of Cornell University's College of Veterinary Medicine. He practices in New Gloucester, Maine, which he characterizes as a rural community. "I bought this equine practice in 1972," he says, "and I've been here ever since."

Dave is not the usual veterinarian—he is interested in chiropractic, acupuncture, homeopathy, as well as such esoteric pursuits as diagnosing and healing animals through thought and feeling. About Kate, he said:

People hear about Kate and call her. It's always with a little I-wonder-if-it's-going-to-work-but-anyway-it'll-be-fun, you know. In my case, it's always horses. She says she'll read the horse and call back. That's usually the way she works. What has been amazing to me is that she really puts herself out on a limb. She'll say things like, "This mare's last baby really bothered her." Things like that. Nobody's ever told her that the mare had a baby at all. I found her very accurate on problems that the horse has. If she says the horse has a back problem, it's the third lumbar that's out, or the feet hurt, it's right on, better than 80 percent accuracy. And of the other 20 percent, sometimes I'll scratch my head and say, "I'm not seeing that." Sometimes I'll say to the owner, "I don't know where this part is coming from, but let's keep an eye on it."

Dr. David Jefferson and a patient

I asked this highly trained and experienced medical man what he thought of nonmedical people doing physical healing. Did he think it effective, a good idea?

"I think it's very effective," he said, "and I have my own theory about it. I think it's prayer."

"Like energy?" I prompted, slightly uncomfortable with the old-fashioned word he had just used.

"No, prayer."

I wouldn't give up. "Prayer is energy, isn't it really?" I insisted.

"Well, I suppose. They visualize the part being well. They see the energy moving. I've had experience here locally with healers who do therapeutic touch. They don't directly touch someone, or an animal, they just run their hand an inch or two over the affected area, and I've seen good results from that. These other people, animal communicators, are just doing it at long distance.

"You know, I think it's something we've all had that we've lost. With the coming of the industrial age, we've relied on technology. Our feelings are pushed down, and so are the insights that we have. I think it's a very natural process and we've just lost it. We're just starting to regain it now, and these people—the animal communicators—are the pioneers. But it's in all of us. It's like Deepak Chopra says, once you accept that, then you're on your way."

I asked Dave how he got this way, what changed him from a conventional horse doctor to a person who talks like this. He mentioned an experience he had had—his first—with an animal communicator, Nancy Regalmuto. I told him that I knew her well, that she certainly was an extraordinary clairvoyant. He agreed and went on:

That was an astounding day. It was over a dozen years ago. That's when I first learned about all this network. I met her at a farm. The owner of this standard breed farm said to me, "I'm having her come, what do you think about that?" He's sort of shuffling his feet. I said, "I'll be interested. That sounds like fun."

It was really astounding. They brought the horses out one at a time. Of course, I knew every one of those horses, what they'd been through. She would tell us about the horses. There was one that had been through a real traumatic incident on the turnpike when a trailer had overturned, and she knew that. Since the wreck, he hadn't been the same. At that time, she was just starting with horses, so she wasn't really good at her anatomy. She'd say, "There's something. It's warm, there's a fuzzy feeling, it's right here on the horse." She said it was the size of an orange. So I did a pregnancy test, and sure enough, the horse is pregnant, and the embryo sac was the size of an orange.

The next one—and I'll never forget this—she said, "The same thing, except this one feels like it's shriveled." And that was a mare who was losing a foal. The foal had died and a lot of material was still in there. So that made me a believer. That was a long time ago. I've always been open to it ever since.

I like stories that involve veterinarians. This one involves animal communicator Sharon Lunde of Prince George, British Columbia, and horse owners Brenda and John Colebrooke, of the same town. The animal is Rafter, a quarter horse gelding.

"Rafter became ill last fall," Brenda told me. "He didn't eat, didn't drink. He was very lethargic, seemed quite uncomfortable. The vet didn't know for sure what his problem was, but it seemed to be some sort of colic. He had abdominal pain, cramping, a high fever. We had to force-feed him, treat him with antibiotics.

"Sharon had worked in the past with Rafter. One night she couldn't sleep, and Rafter came through to her, and she did a healing on him. The next morning I called home from work and my hubby said it seemed like a miracle, but Rafter's fever had broken."

At this point, Brenda mentioned that the hubby was also the vet, which startled me. I wondered how the chips were going to fall on this one. I asked Brenda what Dr. John thought about all this.

"He used to be very skeptical about animal communication," she replied, "but he's seen enough of it to believe that it's real and it works." She also informed me that John was there and would be glad to talk with me. He turned out to be quite willing to consider the possibility that Sharon's long-distance ministrations had had something to do with Rafter's recovery. He said, "I felt that Rafter had probably eaten something that had caused a partial blockage. He had a very high fever. We did blood work and different things, but we couldn't really pinpoint why he was off his food, and he wouldn't drink at all, and he was losing weight. We would support him, I would tube him and give him electrolytes and water by stomach tube. We gave him antibiotics. For several weeks, we weren't sure which way he was going to go. I know Brenda talked with Sharon about him and then he did turn around. It's hard to know whether I did it or she did it."

"That's what people wonder," I said. "Is this sort of healing just hocus-pocus or is there actually something to it?"

"The communicating, I'm convinced, does exist," John said. "We've had many episodes that Sharon has helped us with. One of our dogs, a puppy, got hit by a car and ran off. Sharon told us that the dog was still alive. We thought it might have died; it was gone for two days. Sharon located it telepathically in a farmer's hay bin. I've seen this happen with her a number of times, which makes me wonder if there is much more to it than I understand. But there are a lot of skeptics out there, for sure."

I called Sharon, whom I had interviewed before on other subjects, to get her point of view on Rafter. I also mentioned the case to other animal communicators, who told me it was not unusual for animals to reach out telepathically to communicators with whom they had had former contact.

"Animals do come to you," Sharon told me. "It was about two in the morning. I became very restless; I couldn't sleep. I woke up knowing there was something wrong, I didn't know what. I got up and went into the living room and sat down, and within seconds Rafter was right there with me. I could sense his presence and his thoughts. I had already done some healing on him that day. He had been very, very sick for some weeks. It was a very crucial time. I immediately went into meditation and began sending him as much love as I could. I did that for some time, for probably fifteen or twenty minutes. In the morning, I called Brenda and she said that Rafter's fever had broken in the night and that he was OK. John had been pumping fluids into him, which I'm sure was his saving grace. Between the two of us, and my being able to be with him when he was in great need, he felt fine."

Fay Witherell of Kents Store, Virginia, is a veterinarian who often works with Kate Reilly. She gave me an interesting detective story about how Kate helped when Fay's dog became dangerously ill.

Fay had been in Illinois at a gathering of the American Chiropractic Association. She had her little dog Riggo with her. Riggo was a schipperke, a Belgian barge dog. Riggo needed a comfort stop, so she took him outside. "There was a group of small buildings," she recalls, "with only a foot or two between them, and a cracked cement sidewalk in front of them. I had Riggo on a long leash, and he kept dancing in between these buildings. The grass was all trashed by moles."

After they had returned to Virginia, Riggo got very sick. He was along with Fay when she was doing some house calls, about twenty-five miles from home. She took him to a local veterinary hospital. She had to go on to keep some appointments, so she called Kate and told her about Riggo's illness, and where he was. She told Kate where she would be later in the day. A few hours later, she called the hospital and was told that Riggo had been very sick, but about 2:00 P.M. had taken a turn for the better and was now out of danger. Kate had worked on him from North Carolina about that time. Fay had suspected that Riggo had eaten something poisonous, but she didn't know when or where. And here is where Kate's Sherlock Holmes bit comes in.

"Kate told me," Fay says, "that during her communication with Riggo she was seeing a small shed, and a cement walk with a big crack in it. Then I remembered those sheds. Riggo knew where he had gotten the bad stuff. That was the first that I knew for sure that these communications are for real. It was just dramatic! Since then I've taken workshops with Kate, and I use it myself in my practice."

———

I asked Kate Reilly what percentage of success she felt she had had in her cases. She said she was highly accurate in diagnosis, but that it was difficult to know in regard to healing.

"As far as healing is concerned," she said, "it's like reading two-thirds of a book. I often don't find out how it comes out. People come to my workshops and they know all these stories—what happened—that I don't know about. I hear things like, 'We sat around and we heard Kate Reilly stories.'"

Here are a few more Kate Reilly stories.

———

Jan Spiers of Gordonsville, Virginia, is director of an agency that deals with mental retardation. She has taken courses with Kate and is beginning to practice animal communication, although at the time I talked with her she wasn't charging fees. "I was very surprised by the whole process," she told me, "and how easy it is, and how constantly the communication is available."

Her introduction to communication—and Kate—was, she said, very dramatic.

"The whole idea of animal communication was very new to me. I'd just read a little about it. I was desperate about getting some help with my senior dog. Her name is Chivas, like the scotch."

"Like Chivas Regal?" I asked.

"That's her full name," Jan said. "She was very, very aggressive toward my new puppy; I couldn't let him out of the crate. The puppy's name is Casey. Kate spoke with Chivas telepathically. It was long distance; Kate lived in New Hampshire at the time. It was very evident at our end when Kate was speaking to Chivas. Chivas just quieted right down. And Chivas actually approached the crate and calmly lay down beside it, the crate that held the puppy. It was the first time since the puppy had arrived, three days before, that had happened.

"Kate talked with Chivas about learning to be the new puppy's mother; that was her role now. To help the puppy learn about our family, that she would be like a mother to him, like a teacher. And Kate encouraged us to talk to Chivas in that language. This was in June 1994. And now Chivas and Casey are the best of friends."

Jan went on to relate an example of Kate's diagnosis of physical disease, involving Casey. She told me:

When Casey was six months old I asked Kate to speak to him, just to get to know him better. Because I found the whole thing so fascinating. I didn't have any concerns. At that time he was about seventy pounds, a big puppy. Kate spoke to him again, telepathically. And when she called me back on the phone, she said, "Jan, I think your dog is sick, seriously sick."

I'm watching the puppy running back and forth across the room, jumping over things, a really boisterous puppy. I thought, no way, that's truly wrong.

Kate said, "I think he has disease in the joints." And she listed where she thought the disease was. I was thinking, there's no way, this dog is full of life and vitality. But I decided to take him to the vet. And between that phone call and the time he actually got to see the vet he started limping. And the x-rays confirmed that he had the disease in the joints that Kate had specified, and not in other joints where it more traditionally would be found. It's pretty scary, and it's really amazing. The dog is fine now. He had major surgery and is doing well.

Jan told me another example of Kate's prowess as a diagnostician. "I just took my other dog into the vet yesterday because I thought she had a bladder infection from what Kate had told me when we were doing telepathic communication. And the dog in fact did. But there were no symptoms present, the infection was just at the beginning stage."

"Did the dog know she had a problem?" I asked.

"Oh yeah," Jan replied, "they're very aware. And you can enter their body, which is what Kate does. In the same process of connecting with their thought, you can connect with their body."

The following account from Kate Solisti, a communicator based in Santa Fe, New Mexico, involves both emotional and physical healing, illustrating how closely our bodies and emotions are intertwined. Kate experienced this at the beginning of her career as an animal communicator. She and her husband had moved to Santa Fe and she had become apprenticed to a psychic.

The psychic had sent me on a consultation that involved a golden retriever, about six years old, who was very sick. He had tumors all over his body. The vets had decided that if they tried to cut them out there'd be no dog left. His person was very open to anything that might help.

So I sat with him quietly, and I breathed with him, and just connected with him sort of by instinct, because I didn't have any technique at that point. I asked him if there was anything he could tell us about why he was sick and how we could help him. And instantly, this little movie began to play in my mind.

I saw him, as a puppy, and there were two other puppies, his siblings, and there was this present person who was in the room with us. And she was bathing and brushing and spending all this time and attention on these other two puppies, and leaving him out. What was happening emotionally for him was that he was beginning to feel unimportant, left out, and unloved. And finally, without as much as a good-bye to him, she bundled up the other two puppies and took them off in her car. And at that moment, he decided she didn't love him.

And then it stopped, this little movie. As I had seen it, I told it to the woman, and she said, "Oh my God, I was taking them to the dog show to sell them. And this dog was my favorite; I loved him best and was intending to keep him!"

She burst into tears and threw her arms around his neck and said, "I love you, and if there's anything I can do that will help you stay with me, I'll do it."

And there was a major shift between them, somehow, and within two weeks his tumors were gone.

I commented that if the woman loved the dog so much, she must have sent him good vibes all through his life. Kate replied, "Yes, but as with children, when they're very young and impressionable, if something kind of locks in, it sticks there for a very long time."

Dawn Hayman says, "I don't actually do healing per se, on a professional basis anyway. I work with vets. I'm thinking of one cat in particular who was dying. It had a temperature of 107 and they didn't expect it to live more than twenty-four hours. It had been sick for several days. They'd done all sorts of testing and couldn't find anything wrong with it. The lady gave me a call out of desperation, and her vet, who wasn't particularly open to animal communication, was on the other phone, the extension. They were calling from the vet's office.

"Basically, the cat was telling me he thought it was something he ate. They had already tested for poisoning, they thought he might have eaten a poisonous plant. The cat started telling me when he started feeling

SYLVIA by Nicole Hollander

© 1996 by Nicole Hollander.

bad and what he started to feel. He had started feeling sick before the symptoms showed up to the owner.

"The vet said, 'Excuse me a minute,' and he got off the phone. They called me back the next day. What the cat had said he felt before he started showing symptoms gave the vet one more thing to check on. And it developed that the cat had had an allergic reaction to something that set up a problem in his liver, which caused a condition in his body that they hadn't tested for. When they tested for that, they put him on a very specific antibiotic, and he was better in five hours. He was home the next morning."

Corroboration of diagnoses can come from many sources—in this next case, it came from a videotape. Dawn Hayman told me:

A lady came to me for a consultation because her dog was having trouble in the show ring. He wouldn't sit down for the required amount of time that was necessary to win a ribbon. When I talked with the dog about it, he said that he totally understood what was expected of him but that his hip was bothering him. This was still a very young dog, only about a year old. The dog said that every time he sat down he would get this cramp in his hip. Actually he said it was coming from his neck; he said there was something going on in his neck.

I recommended to his owner that she check with a chiropractic veterinarian. So she did, and sure enough, the dog had pinpointed exactly the right places in his hip and neck. They adjusted the dog, and after that the dog had no problems sitting in the show ring, or anywhere else. He immediately started winning ribbons.

His owner asked me how he had gotten this condition. I asked him about it, and he said he had been born with it. He gave me the image of his being really cramped in the womb. His head was folded underneath one of his shoulders, and when he came out his neck was hurt. His neck was hurt the day he was born. Of course, there's no way to prove that. I got this image from him, and I told the woman.

But she called me the following year. She had been at a dog show. "Somebody recognized my dog," she told me, "and said that she owned one of my dog's littermates. This woman told me that if I ever wanted to see my dog being born, she had it on videotape." So she got the videotape from this other woman and sure enough, right on the videotape the dog comes out and his head is wrapped around his shoulder. He couldn't even turn his head for a half hour after he was born, but nobody noticed it.

———————

Communicator Betty Lewis, who is a registered veterinary technician, had some interesting comments on physical healing. "I do a lot of energy healing," she said. "The only one who can truly heal an individual is that person or animal itself. I can't heal someone else, but I can precipitate healing in someone else by using different forms of energy. I am careful to say that I don't do healing, that I am not a veterinarian, and that I don't contradict anything that a veterinarian tells them to do. But I do explain. Coming from a medical background, I am able to explain a lot why veterinarians say to do certain things. And I can offer alternative solutions, and let the people make the choices based on their own understanding and where they're coming from.

"I use Bach flower remedies, therapeutic touch, and Reiki touch. Bach flowers are the energy of certain plants and flowers, which resonate with the vibrations of human and animal emotions, and balance them."

———————

Dave Jefferson, the open-minded Maine veterinarian, spoke enthusiastically of a young woman in his area who is new to animal communication. "She's one of Kate Reilly's students," he said. "She's very, very talented. She's done some unbelievable stuff."

Melanie Thompson and Geneva

Her name is Melanie Thompson, and she lives in East Baldwin, Maine. She works on a horse farm and gives riding lessons. She studied radio, film, and TV production at Syracuse University, and worked for a short time in that far-from-earthy field. "I just did enough," she says, "to know that I wanted to do riding and teaching more."

She has been doing communication professionally for only about a year but is becoming busier and busier. One of her early patients was her own dog.

"It's an example of energy work making a difference," she told me. "He had a growth between his shoulder blades. It felt like a tumor or a cyst of some kind. I got worried about it. I sort of monitored it for a day or two, and thought I'd bring him to a vet if it didn't get better in a week. And then I decided to do energy work on him. I just decided we weren't going to have a tumor, we were going to be healthy and happy, without little things growing on our bodies. So I did the energy work on it, and it disappeared. It was gone by the fourth day."

"Did you throw thoughts at it?" I asked.

"Basically it's healing with the aura and the energy of the body," she said. "The theory is that when there is disease in the body there is blocked energy. In order to heal, you need to get the energy moving. So with the permission of the universe—you ask the universe to heal the animal—you use your hands to feel where the energy is smooth, or where it feels prickly or blocked. With your hands, you just move the energy around and get it going, so that healing can come to the area."

I asked Melanie for some other examples of her activities.

"A woman called me about a horse," she said. "Dave [Jefferson] had recommended that she call me, because the horse wasn't eating, was pacing in her stall, and was very nervous. She had been that way for about a week. Dave said he couldn't find anything physically wrong with her. I spoke with the horse from my home and found out why she was nervous.

"She had been abused by a number of different owners during her lifetime, and they were all men. There was a new horse in the barn, and the person who owned that horse was a man. And he was coming into the barn at a time when her own person was not present. It was making her very uncomfortable and scared. I told the woman who owned her what was troubling the horse. I used energy work to calm the horse down. I sort of smoothed her aura and tried to get her to relax more. After I had spoken with the horse, her owner went to the barn, and she was calm."

I asked Melanie if she could give me another example of physical healing, and she told me this:

I got a call from a woman last fall who told me her dog wasn't using his hind end at all. He appeared to be paralyzed from about the head back. He wasn't walking, he was just dragging along. The vet had recommended surgery, and the woman was wondering if that was a good decision. I spoke with the dog, who was a medium-size breed. When I went inside his body, it was miserable—his entire spine felt like it was just crunched up. I immediately started doing energy work on it. His body was so tense. As I did the energy work, it started to relax.

When I go inside the animal's body, my body becomes their body. I can do energy work at long distance because my body is their body. If I use my hands along my body, it's going to be affecting their body. I work on my own body. I recommended to the woman that she go to a vet who did some alternative things. I felt that acupuncture would be helpful to the dog. I told the woman to call me if the dog got sick again. I haven't heard from her, and that was six months ago.

I've had wonderful experiences with acupuncture, done by Dave, with my own horses. It's made a tremendous difference in their behavior, attitude, and also in their movement. I do energy work on my horses as well now, and it's helped them.

Melanie told me that her father held a Ph.D. in nuclear physics, and worked in that field near Boston. I asked what he thought of her activities.

"Well," she said, "my mother knows what I'm doing, but I haven't told my father yet because he lives in such a scientific world. I wanted to have enough ammunition, enough examples. Like my dog's tumor going away. Or, 'I knew exactly what this horse was eating for breakfast and dinner, explain that. And not only that, Dad, but I'm getting enough calls now so that I'm able to make a living at it, it's coming to that.' So I've been planning my attack as far as telling him."

––––––––––

"He died a couple of years ago. He was known throughout the world. He was into everything. He believed that not just one thing could heal, that everything was necessary to bring all the points together. He did homeopathy, nutrition, Reiki, acupuncture, laser, crystal therapy, mineral and vitamin supplements. He made up all his own homeopathics, specifics for the animal's blood. If an animal had a tumor, he would take part of that tumor and make a homeopathic out of it to fight it. Or he would use the animal's blood or urine, or whatever."

Who is this paragon of a medical man, this healer we are talking about? Denise Kinch, an animal communicator who lives in Groveland, Massachusetts, on Boston's North Shore, is talking about Dr. Richard Kearns, who for many decades lived and practiced extraordinary veterinary medicine in Hingham, on the South Shore.

"He was eighty-seven when he died," Denise said. "He worked every day till the day before he died. He was a country vet who found that the old ways were really good ways—herbs and Native American remedies, German things like homeopathy. Part of the problem with a lot of holistics nowadays is that they only do one thing. They specialize in homeopathy, or in nutrition, or in acupuncture. But Dr. Kearns used to say, 'You know, it takes the village to heal the animal.'

"I got to know him very well. He wanted me to study with him, but I had really young kids at the time, and it was an hour and a half drive from here. But I was down there every week. I recently read a book that I feel comes the closest I've seen to what Dr. Kearns did. It says that it takes an alignment of everything to get a really true healing. The book is called *Earthway*. It's by Mary Summer Rain.

"Dr. Kearns was an incredible healer, he was the best that we'll ever meet. He used to say, 'Just remember, our animals are here to heal us.'"

The reader is probably aware by now that there is a leitmotiv throughout this book—that animals are sometimes our guardians, sometimes our guides. In one way or another, people kept telling me this. After a while, I began to suspect that it might be true.

"In two weeks," Denise said, "using alternative therapy, Dr. Kearns was able to regenerate my dog's liver to normal size, when conventional vets had given up. She had taken my disease, and she finally died of my disease. It had never manifested in me physically. One's disease is in one's aura, one's luminous body. If it stays there long enough, it manifests in the physical body. The dog would remove it from my luminous body and heal it. I didn't even know it existed."

Denise is one of those people who is born to help animals. "I communicated with animals from an early age," she said. "I used to talk to them in my head, and they would always answer. I shut down for a while because of my upbringing, but I always spent a lot of time with animals and in the woods, much more time than with people. Animals have always been my saving grace. I was always the one who could fix the neighborhood animals. The kids would always bring the hurt birds over, the baby squirrels. I couldn't come home without finding something tied to my back door."

Denise got a degree from the University of Massachusetts in zoology and animal science. She went to Africa in the Peace Corps, and among other things saved the lives of thousands of chickens who had been in the process of being broiled alive, unintentionally, in aluminum chicken coops. "It's 120 degrees during the day there," she says. She helped the Africans with selective breeding, before being invalided back to the United States with lung disease. Some years later, Denise became a master of the energy healing art of Reiki, which she says she used to heal herself.

I suspected that Denise's relationships with conventional veterinarians might be a bit unconventional, and I wasn't mistaken. "There's a fine line to walk with veterinarians," she says. "I've been there. I worked in a conventional veterinary hospital, and ended up being fired because I gave treatments to turn around animals with chronic diseases. I overstepped the conventional bounds and said there is another way. It was time for me to move on anyway.

"But I really don't have problems with veterinarians. Most of the vets in this area know what I do. I work closely with a vet I've known for a long time. I never diagnose. I give suggestions, you don't have to follow them. I offer herbs. I do homeopathy, but only for people I know well. I do flower therapy, and I do crystal healing. I don't heal, I'm a channel for the universe. I do nothing. The universal energy is channeled through me into a client. It works on four levels: physical, emotional, mental, and spiritual. It goes where it's needed."

Denise's small daughter had just come home from school, not feeling well. Denise had taken her into her lap as we went on with the interview. She put her hands on the little girl's knee, saying, "If I put my hands on her knee, the energy enters, but it goes to her shoulder, her stomach, I have no way of telling it where to go. It knows where it needs to go. No matter what you do, it can do no harm."

One of the constant threads I was aware of in my research was that we all seem to have powers that we don't suspect; we can all do these things, perhaps with some instruction and effort. Carol Gurney, a well-known communicator based in Agoura, California, gave me yet another instance of this concept. She told me:

There was this seventeen-year-old Lhasa apso who was incontinent, could barely move, and was not eating. The vet suggested to its owner that she put the dog down. The owner called me and said, "We are willing to put the dog down, but we want to know what the dog wants." At long distance, I asked the dog what he wanted to do. He said he was not ready to go, that he was not finished with his job with the family. I had the strongest feeling that I should go there and do some hands-on work with the dog.

When I got out there I realized what the dog was trying to tell me about not wanting to leave. The woman was paralyzed. She had had an aneurysm while giving birth and was still somewhat paralyzed on her left side. The dog didn't want to leave until the woman had recovered.

I did some work with the dog. I just scanned his body. I went over his body energetically to see where the energy was not moving, or where there was too much energy. I wanted to show the woman how to do this with her dog. I worked with her this day, and she caught on tremendously. She was able to feel where there was too much energy and where there was no energy. She called back a couple of days later and said, "My dog is now in the backyard running around, he's eating, going to the bathroom. When we go out, he's at the front door wagging his tail."

The woman, with some instruction from Carol, had been able to help her dog significantly. He lived for another year. This was not only helpful to the dog, Carol adds, but also to the woman.

"By her doing this energy work," Carol said, "it helped her. That is part of healing when we do body work. By his staying alive, it kept her stronger. If he had died then, it would have been a very inappropriate time to leave for her, because she was so bonded with him."

Sibly Hannigan, a riding instructor who lives in Harvard, Massachusetts, has dealt with horses since she was six years old. She has recently studied communication with Kate Reilly.

"Kate did a body read on each of us in a workshop," she said. "She told me that breathing in was more difficult for me that day than breathing out, and I did get a cold in three days. When I did reads on other people or horses, I got definite sensations about posture, weight bearing, shin splints, and so on. And I was right on the money. I told a woman she had lifts in her shoes, and there was no way I could know that.

"I know that the energy work Kate has taught us absolutely works. She has shown us how to use our hands for healing and energy massage. I use it on my own horse and I can see the results in him. With another horse, I diagnosed a pulled groin muscle and helped heal it, and I showed her owner how to do it. This work is daisy-chaining, there is a huge spiritual awakening within the horse community. My own vet has actually admitted that he does this sort of stuff. When you work around animals, you've got to have some sort of psychic ability; they don't talk to you, you've got to read 'em."

Sibly told me she can get messages from animals through words and sensations.

"I haven't had a bolt of lightning out of the sky," she says. "I just know the stuff works. You can truly help with the healing of animals through psychic work. I'm just learning. But it's not learning, it's something that I'm getting in touch with, it's been there all along."

One of the most interesting and informative interviews I did while researching this book was with Dr. Judith Shoemaker of West Grove, Pennsylvania, a widely known and highly regarded veterinarian. She graduated as a vet from the University of Georgia in 1980, and for ten years had a conventional practice. Since then she has been closely involved with alternative therapy. She is licensed in twelve states. Her practice now leans heavily on chiropractic and acupuncture, and she estimates that she has the largest practice of this variety in the country. But she also still practices conventional veterinary medicine.

"I'm not out there on a limb with Shirley MacLaine," she says. "I have to be very legitimate. I have to work in concert with conventional veterinarians because of the caliber of the horses that I work with. I work on some of the top horses in every discipline. The therapy center in which I work is considered to be the best at what it does. We work on all the horses on the Olympic team. I worked this morning on the fastest trotting colt of all time. He's been a patient of mine since he was very small."

Judith has taken workshops with Jeri Ryan, one of the top animal communicators, whom she praises as "a psychologist and very, very well-educated woman. She's very, very good at what she does. She's always overwhelmed with work because she is so accurate."

In working on such a right-brained book as this one, I am always delighted to run across scientists—left-brainers—who confirm what I am writing about. Judith certainly fits this bill; she can even trace it to her ancestry. "My father was a mechanical engineer and a career Air Force officer," she told me. "He was pretty left-brain. I tell you, my father was the most logical human being that ever was."

She has never married. "Animals are my livelihood and my family," she said. "What I consider a very spiritual vocation is what I get to make a living at."

I had first heard about Judith from animal communicator Anita Curtis of Gilbertsville, Pennsylvania. Judith in turn told me many interesting things, a couple of them about Anita. One of her anecdotes illustrates how communicators can work in conjunction with professional veterinarians. Here is the anecdote, as told to me by Judith:

A horse had been admitted to the clinic for a ligament tear. He had been treated conventionally and was there for us to do our electromagnetic therapy stuff. Anita was walking down the aisleway and went by this horse and she said she heard him say that his stomach hurt, that he had a terrible stomachache. The horse didn't look like he was colicky; he didn't show any kind of pain whatsoever. But the next day when we cleaned his stall we found that his manure smelled very, very bad. It smelled like carnivore poop, which meant that he perhaps had some blood in his stool. Because normally, ruminant poop does not smell very bad. Horses are not ruminants, but they are herbivores and they don't eat meat. When you get that in an herbivore it usually indicates that they have ulcers and they're bleeding into their gut. Horses that have ulcers often are extremely anemic, and when we did his blood work it was indeed evident that he was anemic. He had been treated conventionally for the ligament tear with bute, which is an anti-inflammatory drug and can cause ulcers. We didn't know him from Adam, and he was showing no signs of pain when we looked at him. But he had said to Anita that he had stomach pain. And when we then treated him for an ulcer his poop cleaned up immediately. And his demeanor improved, which would indicate that his pain had been chronic because of this stomach ulcer. He'd learned to cope with it, but he certainly felt much better when he didn't have it. Anita was just walking down the aisleway, but she can do this at a distance, she doesn't have to be with the animal.

I mentioned to Judith that I was emphasizing in the book that one did not have to be an extraordinary psychic to practice effectively as an animal communicator, that I was constantly being told that all of us are psychic and that we can develop the ability.

"Exactly," Judith answered. "Anita is the most down-to-earth, regular, everyday kind of individual that ever walked. She's just a little old person. She's been ill and had ups and downs, but life experience is all part of developing the sense that there are better ways of connecting. She's a perfect example of a very normal human development and having it extend into what we think is a paranormal type of situation. And it is not; it is simply an extension into simple humanness. Or animalness, the simple connectedness that all animals share.

"I have a very interesting practice because I have to teach animals to let me adjust them. I do that with a great deal of mental imagery. After I work with a horse I can ask it to do things to prove to its owner that these things are true, like ask it to put its ears in a certain way, or shut its eyes, or pick up its hoof. And they do it. I do very similar things to what Anita does in that I often just get a feeling in my body about certain things that may be wrong with the animals.

"Anita comes down many times to our clinic to check herself against our diagnostic work," Judith went on. "She will ask the animal what's going on with it, where it hurts, what's happening, how it feels. What they tell her is then put against what we've felt it is. Sometimes she does this before we see the horse, sometimes after. It lines up very consistently. She's been terrifically accurate. Many times she's found out some-

Anita Curtis with BB

thing that we didn't know and then we go look for it, and it actually is there. That's been very helpful for many owners, because a lot of times conventional diagnostic work can be just sort of poke and hope."

———————

I asked Judith what she thought about lawsuits, presumably involving practicing medicine without a license, that had been brought against animal communicators by veterinarian groups. She said there could be two sides to the matter, that sometimes the communicators were not only diagnosing but treating the animals by such means as homeopathics, and sometimes they were not fully qualified to do this, and this could be a danger. But she indicated that it was a variable and complicated question.

"Sometimes," she said, "the veterinarians are very threatened by the abilities of a communicator who may be extremely accurate. Sometimes it becomes a big moneymaking deal, and that is the vets' upset. But sometimes a communicator will tell an owner, 'Your animal will not get better if you do the regular, conventional stuff, it will only get better if you do this.' And that is a danger if the animal has something that is only helped by conventional medicine. That's why a case could be instituted about practicing veterinary medicine without a license. There's a combination of several levels and interaction. I believe terrifically in what many animal communicators do. They can be very, very accurate, and they have the best interest of the animals in mind. But again, if one starts to mix the apples and oranges of consciously sought profit, then that would be something resented by veterinarians, and it may cloud the issue. I believe communicators should be able to make a living at doing this. I believe totally in that. But one has to make sure that one's intent stays appropriate."

I asked Judith about lawsuits that had been filed by veterinarians against communicators.

"Some of them have been legitimate." she said. "Veterinary laws in every state say that practice of veterinary medicine constitutes diagnosis and treatment of ailments and afflictions. So if someone gets to the point where they would exclude conventional medicine, then it may become a danger to the public."

I asked her, "What do you feel, then, are 'illegitimate' lawsuits?"

She replied, "I think when somebody is doing it because they are bent out of shape because their diagnosis was not as accurate as the psychic's. And I find that's very frequent. There are plenty of people who pooh-pooh the psychics because they're feeling a little sour grapey, because they got upstaged.

"I don't feel there's any problem with animal psychics doing their work so long as they know that they have a sympathetic practitioner who will give credence to what they say and use it as additional diagnostic information. Animal communicators can couch language in a way that serves both their business and their intent but also would not interfere with the appropriate practice of veterinary medicine. Then they would not get in a pickle as far as diagnosing, prescribing, and whatever."

Veterinarian Fay Witherell has taken seminars with Kate Reilly, does psychic communication with animals, and also uses homeopathy. She says:

A lot of veterinarians are hostile to anything they don't know and understand. A lot of them are terrified of all this stuff, because they see us curing animals that they can't cure and they don't understand it at all. I'm talking not only about veterinarians, but also M.D.s. The holistic veterinarians are reluctant to take on a case if there is an M.D. in the extended family, because there will be a hostile takeover of your case somewhere along the way. That's happened to me. I didn't realize that the guy running the horse barn was a retired M.D.

The AVMA (American Veterinary Medical Association), they've still got their heads stuck in the sand. They do acknowledge acupuncture. That involves sticking needles into things, so they think they should own that. So they don't like laypeople going around sticking needles in. They've still got their heads stuck in the sand about chiropractic. And homeopathy. They go so far as to take the homeopathic medicines and analyze them. If you know about homeopathy, you know that you're only dealing with the energy of the medicine, you have diluted the original substance to the point where there's not a molecule of it left, and then you imbue these little sugar pills with this energy. It's very potent stuff. People will spend thousands of dollars x-raying, ultrasounding, doing all these tests on a horse, trying to figure out what's wrong with it, and then somebody a thousand miles away says, it's not your horse's left ankle that's bothering him, it's the right side of his pelvis and his lumbars are out. The conventional practitioners are just not going to hear this.

Some animal communicators are better than others. It bothers me when they start prescribing homeopathics, because to do homeopathy correctly you have to go into a case with pretty much an open mind. Any one of at least hundreds of remedies might be the one to choose, and these people, most of them, have limited knowledge of a limited number of remedies, and they think of them in an allopathic way. So I have trouble with the ones who do this. But diagnostically, a good communicator like Kate is incredible.

I only use psychic communication and healing when I have a client who I know will be open. I will ask, "Do you mind if I try psychically to find out where it hurts?" Although without doing it consciously, I think I do it on a lot of animals I treat, and a lot of them get more better than I think they should, than you'd expect right off. And if I have the owner's permission, I'll work on their bodies at home at night.

All of the holistic people say that it's the intent that's the most important. Whether they know it or not, that's psychic healing, the intent. It's that same intent of a little girl who goes out to the barn and hugs her sick pony. She has done an incredible psychic healing right there. How many times have doctors—especially the old-time doctors—said it's the nursing that's so important. That nurse is just full of psychic intent. They do it without even thinking about it. When you are beside something that's sick and you really care about it, that goes over. It's easy for me to go out to my horse that I just love more than anything and do a total body energy job on him, give him everything. And then you might go out to a client with a testy old dog who stinks and is trying to bite you every time you turn around, but you have to care about it as much—as an animal, as a soul, as a being, as a patient—and treat it with total love.

You have to remind yourself of that a little bit. But these healers, these true doctors and nurses, and these little girls who run out and just fill their ponies with love when they're sick, that's what really helps. What they're doing is psychic healing.

7

Workshops That Can Train You in Animal Communication

I would suspect that the readers of this book, having read this far, have begun to wonder if they themselves could do some animal communication. I certainly wondered if I could. I was not too optimistic, for although I am aware that in theory I am psychic, in practice I have never had much luck. I've tried taking out-of-body trips at the Monroe Institute in Virginia, where they pipe differently pitched sounds into your ears to create a "window." Although within a few days practically everybody else in the class was through the window and flying all over this dimension and a few others, my own psyche remained stuck in my body as though by some cosmic glue.

I joined a workshop at a Spiritualist church. They put me in an advanced class because I had written books about ghosts. They soon found out that I just *wrote* about ghosts—I couldn't see them or hear them, I just interviewed people who could. The Spiritualists were too polite to demote me to an entry-level class, but I quit from sheer inferiority feelings.

I might create minimal suspense in the reader by going directly from here to my adventures in animal communication workshops. Did this guy finally have a breakthrough, the reader would wonder. If *he* could do it, *anyone* can. But that would result in something of a letdown, for I didn't have any extraordinary experiences, just a few ordinary ones, the kind we ordinary folk pass off as coincidence, lucky guesses. But I think the animal communicators are right, we ordinary people can learn to do it right if we just give it a determined try.

In everyday, person-to-person communicating, most of us are up in our heads, very left-brain and analytical. But to do *real* communication with nonhumans—or for that matter, with humans—you've got to have heart, as the old Broadway show tune put it. An extraordinary clairvoyant and animal diagnostician, Nancy Regalmuto, told it to me this way: "An artist painted a picture of Jesus knocking on a door. People who saw the painting said, 'It's not finished, there's no doorknob on the door.' The artist replied, 'That door is to the human heart, it can only be opened from the inside.'"

Nancy went on, "You have to open your heart when you work with animals. You have to allow yourself to be vulnerable. You have to allow love to be exchanged between yourself and the subject. It is essential that the heart chakra be opened, because animals have a very highly developed love nature. That's how they connect with humans; that's how they come into humans. And if you're not going to open up that heart chakra to them, to understand them, to love them, to appreciate them, to feel compassion for them, you're not going to be able to reach the energy vibration necessary to connect.

"We all can do it, these are divine rights. We're all coming from the same creator, the same place. We're all the same essentially in our makeup, we all have the same abilities, the same rights. But a lot of people have given up their rights. They don't even know what their rights are.

"You have a right to be able to communicate with all things that God created. This is our divine right. A lot of people think, You can do it, Nancy, because you're gifted. Well, you're gifted too, it's just that you don't recognize your gifts. Those gifts are under all our Christmas trees. I just opened mine."

Janet Shepherd of Haymarket, Virginia, has long been a trainer of horses and a teacher of riding. She gradually became certain that horses talked with each other.

"You could see them put their heads together and decide on something and then act on it. I felt there was something there, but I didn't know what it was."

A professional psychic who talked with animals came to a barn where Janet kept her horse, and gave a demonstration with several horses. "I was pretty sure right away that this was genuine, that she was not a charlatan," Janet relates, "and I was also aware that I was getting some of the things that maybe she wasn't saying out loud."

She began working with this woman, and later with Marlene Sandler, who helped her develop many of the skills she needed to do animal communication, perhaps the most important being meditation. Janet told me:

I worked at meditation. I was doing the kind where you count your breath, but I never felt I was expanding to higher levels of consciousness. However, I did feel I was calming myself and that my brain waves were changing—into the alpha state or whatever. My breathing would slow down and my heart rate would slow down. But I have to admit I was real bored doing it. But there are other ways to meditate. There's meditation in motion. It's good for people who are physically active, as I am. You climb mountains and swing from trees and I don't know what all. Then there's the technique of counting down and going into a light hypnotic state, so that you have some access to your unconscious—to feelings that you might not be aware of, including your psychic abilities.

Our left brain is talking to us all the time, it never stops, but there's a lot of intuitive stuff that is constantly going through our minds. I think we hear it, but it's quite subtle and we don't pay any attention to it, or we dismiss it as our imagination. The left-brain voice is shouting at you, nagging you all the time; the intuitive voice is softer than a whisper.

I meet people every day who are quite telepathic and talk with their animals and don't even know it. I can tell when they are actually communicating with the animals, now that I've developed my own ability. People say to me, "It's so wonderful that you can do this," and I'm able to tell them honestly, "*You* can do this. In fact, you're already doing it, you're just not aware of it."

One spring Saturday I drove from my home near Boston down to Connecticut. A communicator I had interviewed, Nedda Wittels, was giving a one-day workshop on animal communication. The session was held in a rural area south of Hartford, in the house of Deb Dickerson, who had offered her home for the class. We started about 9:00 A.M. and went through till 5:00 P.M. There were five participants, not counting Nedda and myself—four women and one man.

I soon realized these were dedicated animal people. I like animals, myself—sometimes even feel love for them—but it's a casual thing. In my adult life, I've only had one cat and one dog, and they were my wife's idea. But these people *loved* animals. They were emotionally *involved* with them. Most of them had several. In both this gathering and one I attended a few weeks later, I felt almost like an interloper. I didn't *belong* in this crowd. I was there to work, to report, and that was it. When we had our breaks and everyone else was chattering on about the latest cute thing their critters had done, I was gobbling up all the refreshments in sight— largely out of boredom.

Nedda opened the day with a short pep talk. "Everybody who comes to these workshops is doing some level of communication with animals," she said, "because they already have the connections, the love, the experience of being with animals, and when you're with them you learn to communicate. What happens in these workshops is that your consciousness expands. We are all telepathic, but we were taught as kids not to use this skill, not to develop it. People can incorporate this into their daily lives; it's like riding a bicycle, playing the violin."

When I went to the Monroe Institute to learn how to do out-of-body trips and couldn't have any, I interviewed everybody else in the class, since I had agreed to write an article about the place and I was desperate. I found that about 80 percent of the group had had out-of-body experiences before they ever got there. It was the same with both animal communication workshops I attended—almost all of the people had already communicated telepathically with animals. They were just learning more about it, learning to really believe they were doing it.

Nedda asked us to tell a bit about ourselves, why we were there. I was particularly struck with what one of the women said:

I went into a frozen place after my divorce. A cat came into my life, and we developed this psychic connection. I would know, for example, when he was outside wanting to come in. I began to get sentences from him. One time, he said, "I will never see Amy again." Amy is my daughter. It turned out that he was dying, and that was why he wouldn't see her again. When he died, I allowed myself to feel grief for the first time in my life. His name was Speaker.

Deb Dickerson said, "I feel connected when I have an animal companion. There's one horse I haven't been able to make a bond with. I want to find out from her why, what's wrong."

Alex Kozman, who works with Deb (they are police officers at a state mental hospital), had brought along his little dog, Robert Anne, a female Norwich terrier. "I've had dogs since I was a child," he said. "I overlook all my allergies to have my dog with me. I'm here because we want to take the relationship to the next step."

Nedda was using a course developed by Penelope Smith, with whom she had trained. Dawn Hayman, whose workshop I attended subsequently, also used Smith's course. Nedda asked us to be emotionally peaceful, to imagine what it is like to communicate clearly with animals, what it is like to receive and give messages without difficulty, with no barriers. To be open, and ready for surprises.

She had us break up into pairs, and tell our partners verbally about a time an animal had made an impression on us. My partner was a lady with the graphic name of Sandy Beach. Sandy told me about nursing a dog that had cancer, and how she had felt she had to help it die. "In her face," Sandy said, "you could see she so wanted to snuggle, but she couldn't breathe."

I told about how my Irish setter, Seyde, always snuggled against me when we started out in my car.

Nedda asked us to recall a time when an animal had received a thought from us. I told Sandy about the many times when Seyde would know—in fact, slightly before I consciously knew—that I was going to take her for a walk. She'd be at the door, panting, way ahead of me.

Sandy told me that she would let her dog out early in the morning for a comfort stop. Often, instead of coming right back, the dog would visit neighbors. One morning, when Sandy had to leave quickly, she sent this thought to her dog: If you're not back in sixty seconds, you're going to have to sit out here in the cold until my husband gets up. The dog was back at the door in thirty seconds.

We were asked to recall a time when an animal displayed real affection for us. I remembered Seyde's greeting to me when I returned home after an absence of several months. She flew six feet through the air and landed—all seventy-five pounds of her—in my arms.

Sandy recalled that when her mother became sick, her horse, Joey, came over to her and put his head on Sandy's shoulder. Joey had never done that before.

Nedda began to move us into various exercises in telepathy. "These exercises are from human to human," she said. "They are from the heart chakra."

We worked at the telepathic transmitting of colors. At one point, Nedda sent out orange.

Alex got it. "I worked very hard," he told the group, "to keep my doors—my heart chakra—open."

I had gotten orange myself, and I don't even much like the color orange. Just a guess?

I sent my favorite color, lavender, to Sandy Beach. She didn't get it. So who's perfect?

We began to work with photographs of animals that people had brought. I was given a photo of Deb's horse, Mick. I asked Mick for answers to questions proposed by Nedda:

What do you like to eat?
Peppermint, Mick said.
What do you like to do most?
Run.
What makes you angry?
Other animals that get Deb's attention.
Where do you like to go?
All the trails.
How old are you?
Twelve years old.

Deb said the answers I received were right on, but I'm far from sure it was Mick speaking. Could it have been me, guessing well?

Other people got more specific answers. After the sessions, I phoned people and asked them what they got from the workshop. Alex told me of getting answers from Sandy's dog, Tara. One question was, what is your favorite food? Tara said, beef. In answer to a question about her favorite activity, Tara replied, playing in the swamp. Alex said that he hadn't known there was a swamp across the street from Sandy's house.

"I went in very skeptical," he told me, "figuring I had nothing better to do with seventy-five dollars, so let me see if it works and if I can do it. The color thing was easy for me to do. That helped me to think that maybe there is something to this thing, maybe it can be done. As the day went on, I let my skepticism drop a little bit. What I needed was confirmation from somebody else that the answers I got were real, as opposed to doing it with my own dog, when I know the answers he would give. But by the end of the day I felt comfortable that I had some level of ability."

Some of the people said they had gotten words; others said they'd had pictures; and still others said that they'd gotten emotions. Some had gotten a mixture of all three. I found that Sue Huggins, a social worker, had some of the most convincing experiences. She had had a lot of psychic training over the past ten years, she told me. (She also told me I had done well with a photo of her cat, Silky. But you can't prove it by me.)

Sue did some work with a picture of Sandy's horse, Joey. Joey was a joker, a regular card, always had been, Sandy informed us after Sue gave her report.

"I got some of the most outlandish responses from him," Sue told me. "He kept wanting to pull my leg."

She asked Joey what his favorite food was, and he said, "Horse meat."

"That could be your imagination," I said.

"I know," she said.

But some of her conversation with Joey seemed quite evidential. She asked what made him angry, and he replied that it was when the stall door was closed. Sandy later told us that in the winter the lower half of the stall door was closed to keep out the cold air. Maybe Joey was claustrophobic.

Sue asked Joey where he liked best to go, and he replied to the sand, and Sandy said that was true—he liked to roll in sand.

Sue asked what he liked best to eat, and Joey said beans. Sandy said she'd been feeding him meal that looks like beans.

Sandy told me that Joey was also having fun with one of the other women in the group. "He was playing the joker," Sandy said, "giving all kinds of funny answers. He told this woman that he was aching all over— his back hurt, his hip hurt, his leg hurt. She asked him what hurt the most and he said his left front leg, but not to worry because plenty of cookies would take care of it."

All of the people told me that they felt the workshop made them more confident that they had not been imagining the communication they'd had with animals. Deb Dickerson said, "I now feel I can put a little more stock in what I think I'm getting from animals. I've had these feelings for a long time. A workshop like this sort of validates it. I'm going to practice. I'm going to give more credence to the feelings I've had in the past."

Speaking of practice, Nancy Regalmuto had some perceptive words. "I was a bodybuilder for a long time," she told me, which was rather startling. She doesn't *look* like a bodybuilder, although I'm no expert on lady bodybuilders. Nancy is a slim, comely, even ethereal-looking young woman. She told me:

Developing psychic abilities is like bodybuilding. We lift heavier and heavier weights to develop the physical body. This can be equated to psychic ability, to asking more and more and more and more questions. Doing the chiseling work, the refining work. You might be talking with a dog you don't know, someone else's dog. Perhaps a squirrel or a fish. That increases your communications muscle, builds the bulk. Rather than just asking your pet how he feels today, if he likes his food, you're getting into more complex communication.

Progress probably won't happen overnight. But it *might* happen overnight. Your thoughts shape your life. Many people fail to listen. When I was a little girl I was very frightened of people. I just stood around and listened a lot. But if you don't develop your abilities to listen to your fellow human beings, you're not going to listen very well to animals.

Listening is an act of the ear and the heart. Many times animals say to me, "I don't know how many times I've said that to her, but she's not listening." That's where animals are coming from—they feel we're not listening. Listening requires a lot of patience, concentration, and instinct. Listening to your basic instincts, your first impressions. People say, "I should listen to myself a little better," and that's right. You should be open to accept the information you get. It will be disorganized at first, but you have to trust that your brain can integrate these flashes in a way that you can understand.

After you have the motivation, it leads to a commitment. But even a commitment can be shallow if you don't work toward keeping it and developing it.

———

Dawn Hayman began the three-day workshop I attended by mentioning that she had read that the idea that dogs are smarter than cats is not true. She said she had never thought so anyway, but in any case don't tell that idea to a cat.

It reminded me that some years ago I had read that dogs were smarter than cats, and had told my wife about it in the presence of our dog, Seyde, and our cat, Pooka. I was writing a newspaper column at the time. I wrote in my column that ever since I'd mentioned the supposed superiority of dogs over cats, Pooka had been drooping around sullenly and Seyde had been absolutely insufferable.

We used to think that the mere idea that animals could understand us was hilarious. Not so anymore.

Early in the workshop, Dawn mentioned that Captain Zero, one of the cats at the place, a not-for-profit animal shelter called Spring Farm CARES, had been killed on the road a couple of days before. His sister was Sonya Pia, who was considered, by herself and everybody else, as the top cat on the premises. "We haven't seen Sonya Pia for the past couple of days," Dawn told us. "She's all right, but she's mourning."

As casually as that, Dawn indicated that she knew telepathically where Sonya Pia was, and her emotional state. Such communication is a given at Spring Farm CARES. "Your animals at home know where you are and what you are doing," she told the group.

The shelter was founded some years ago by Dawn and her partner, Bonnie Reynolds, on a farm that has been in the Reynolds family since 1802, at Clinton, New York. They care for some 170 animals—horses, llamas, chickens, ducks, cats, dogs, guinea pigs, and rabbits. "Everything," Dawn says. "Once here, they have a place for life."

In November 1993 they suffered a disastrous fire. A barn burned and seventeen cats, four dogs, and five parakeets died. Dawn and Bonnie lost almost everything in the fire; there was no insurance. However, grants and donations have enabled the construction of a fine new building, where the workshop was held, and Spring Farm CARES continues.

Dawn is a widely known animal communicator, a psychic from child-hood who was turned on to working with animals when she read Penelope Smith's books and heard her tapes.

"I realized these were things I had done since I was a kid," Dawn told me. "I thought it was something everybody did. Somewhere along the line while growing up, I learned to shut it off, but it opened up very quickly for me. I started doing it with our animals here, and now I get calls from all over the world. I was doing seventy-five consultations a week but have cut back. You can get too tired doing that many.

"Everybody has the ability to do this, everybody is telepathic, so it's not teaching people to be telepathic, it's teaching people how to recognize that they already are. That's what the focus of this workshop is."

A few days after the workshop, I phoned most of the ten people who had been in the group, and found almost unanimous enthusiasm. I myself had felt that Dawn was spending too much time on stories of her own experiences, and too little on training exercises on how to accomplish telepathy, but I got little support for this opinion. Almost everyone felt that the stories gave them confidence that this could be done.

"You have to believe in something before you can make it a part of your life," Dawn had said.

My problem was that I had been working on this book for about a year and a half, and had already heard dozens of stories, including some of Dawn's. I was already convinced.

When we began exercises, on Saturday afternoon, that would hopefully lead to the development of telepathy, we followed the Penelope Smith pattern, such as sending and receiving colors, and telling each other of experiences with animals. But the main feature of the workshop was direct contact with animals. Dawn would send us out into Spring Farm's buildings to try to telepathize with the animals. Then we would come back to the meeting room and discuss what success or lack of it we'd had.

During the exercises, I had teamed up with a Canadian couple. Jack Frith was a heavy-equipment operator who admitted that he was dubious about communicating with animals, that he had driven down from north of Toronto just to keep his wife, Diane, company. Diane was a systems analyst in a bank. When I interviewed Jack a few days later, he told me he wasn't totally convinced, that it didn't work for him. But Diane was sold on the workshop and was planning to sign up for another with Dawn a few months hence.

"I think I've always been able to communicate," she told me, "but I didn't recognize what was happening. I seem to know what my animals want, to go out, or a cookie, but now I think I'm picking up what they're asking."

The Friths and I had wandered around the big barn. My favorite animal was Tyler the goat. He really seemed to like me. He kept sticking his huge horns through the wooden bars in front of his stall to get closer. I was afraid he was going to get them tangled. I felt we were having communication, that we were pals, but I couldn't for the life of me figure out what he might be trying to tell me.

Diane told me that Tyler had said to her, "Nobody talks to my sister, Tippy. Can't you talk to her?"

I had hardly noticed the tiny goat in the next stall. I thought she was just a kid. I had felt she wouldn't have much to say even if I could hear her, so I gave her a brush-off, and this was apparently riling her loving brother, Tyler.

The Friths and I also hobnobbed with Gulliver, a very large llama. He had huge, soulful eyes. Gulliver and I held eye contact for several minutes. I'm almost sure Gulliver was reading my mind, but I'm darned if I could read his. Diane had met Gulliver before. She told me that this time he said to her, referring to Jack, "Oh, he's with you. That's OK."

Hallie McEvoy had come to upstate New York from northern Vermont. I was slightly surprised when she told me she had started her working life as a cop in Burlington. She certainly seemed feminine, warm, and friendly for a cop. She is now a horse show judge, licensed by the American Horse Show Association. She also writes about horses, and has managed large barns of fifty to a hundred horses. I asked what she thought of the workshop.

"I thought it was great," she said. "I loved the exercises, but I also needed to hear Dawn's stories, because they confirmed something deep inside of me; they rang true for me."

She had had similar experiences, she said, and it seemed obvious from her input during the group discussions that she was telepathic.

It struck me that all of the women at this workshop were psychic, were already animal communicators. They probably didn't particularly need exercises.

"I wanted confirmation that I'm not the only one," Hallie told me. "I wanted more channels opened up. In the past, sometimes I would hear and sometimes I wouldn't. Now I'm much more open."

I asked Hallie how she received animal communication.

"I either see a picture in my head, or it's a voice," she replied.

"Your own voice?" I asked.

"No."

"What kind of voice?"

"A light voice."

"A feminine voice?"

"No, actually it's gender neutral. It's usually that voice, but occasionally a different voice. It's kind of a sing-songy voice. I've been hearing it since I was a kid."

Hallie gave two accounts at the group debriefing sessions of her encounters with the barnyard animals. One was amusing; the other was poignant and mystical. Both were corroborated by Dawn. Hallie seemed to be getting information from the animals in a way that was parapsychological; it seemed very unlikely she would know these things about the animals and the occurrences she related through ordinary channels of communication.

"I'll start with the pony," Hallie told us. "I first went out to the barn on Friday night. The pony said, 'Would you get some food for me? What's taking so long?' I said, 'I can't bring you food, I don't work here.' She said, 'Well, could you ask them to bring it?' Then she said, 'I should be fed first anyway. I am a duchess.' She went on to say, 'Tell Dawn my right eye is bothering me, the same problem I had last year. It's nothing serious, it's a scratch or an allergy. Please tell her I want a boric acid solution put in my eye.' Then she said, 'Look at the left side of my neck. I'm afraid I have the start of a sarcoma there.'"

Dawn told us that although the pony's eye looks normal, she had some sort of illness or trauma involving her eye last year. Dawn also mentioned that the people with whom the pony had been staying recently were afraid that she might be prone to sarcoma, and they had used that word around her.

Hallie said, "I asked her if I could come back and talk with her, and she said, 'Of course, sweetie, did you think this was just a one-time thing?'"

Dawn told us that the pony's name was Dulcie, but she likes to call herself Duchess.

Hallie then told us of her second experience. "The next day, on the way out to talk to Duchess, I felt compelled—or called—to talk to two ducks who were sitting on top of a ramp that went up to the site of the barn that had burned. As I started to walk up the ramp to them, the ducks said, 'Stay back, this is a sacred place. We are the sentinels to guard the sacred place. Many died here. There is still much pain, but it is getting better.'

"I tried moving forward because I wanted to look over the edge of the ramp, but they told me not to. They said, 'We must guard this place, it is our turn. It is cold, and we'd rather be inside, but we must stay here to do our watch.'"

When Hallie told this to the group, other people said they had also heard the animals refer to the burned barn site as the sacred place, and Dawn said that was what the animals called it.

———

Norma Harris is a tall, attractive woman who lives in Bedminster, New Jersey. Her occupation involves advising auto dealers on training, sales, management, advertising, and controlling inventory.

"Dawn's stories were validations for us," she told me. "We had never heard stories like this. It was important for us in order to have the confidence that we could do it. I had never had the experience of having an animal speak back to me, and it was phenomenal. I never had considered that my animals could communicate with me telepathically. I will be doing another workshop with Dawn this summer, without a doubt."

Norma told the group of her experience with Sonya Pia, whose brother, Captain Zero, had been killed by a car a few days before:

> I went out to the barn certain I was going to make a connection with a horse. A cat came up to me and said, "Hi." It was words; it wasn't just a feeling. I didn't hear a different voice, as though it was coming from someplace else. It was like my own voice—in my head. We sat and had a wonderful communication.
>
> It was a big orange cat. I had had an orange cat, and I'm separated from my husband and he had refused to allow me to take my cat, and that was a big issue for me. So it was emotional for me to sit there with an orange cat. I sat there and told this cat that I liked orange cats and I missed mine. And that I hoped my cat knew that I hadn't left him by choice. And this cat very clearly told me not to worry, that my cat understood. When I talked with Dawn and asked her to communicate with my cat, she said he understood completely why he wasn't with me, and that it was OK. I had no idea how old this cat—Sonya Pia—was, and I asked her age and she told me. I asked Dawn, and she said yes, that was the cat's age.
>
> I went to see that cat every day. And when I was leaving the place, after the Tellington TTouch workshop the next week, I didn't see her around. I was getting ready to drive out, when I saw her sitting under a fence, up a little hill. I walked over and asked her if she was going to come down the hill to see me, and she said no. I thought that meant she wanted me to come up, and when I did she turned and ran away. This cat had always run to me, not away. For eleven days, she had come running to me. When I asked her what was the matter, she said it was too sad, she couldn't say good-bye. She said she had just lost her brother, and she had to say good-bye to him, and that it was too hard to say good-bye to me.
>
> I told Sonya Pia that we would always have this connection. No matter where I was, we would always be friends. She said she understood that, she just couldn't say good-bye.

I was intrigued with the similarity of the people in both of the workshop groups I had attended, how they immediately seemed so bonded, and so already attuned to animal communication. I called Denise Kinch of Groveland, Massachusetts, an excellent psychic and animal communicator who lives not far from me and whom I had interviewed at some length. I told her of my adventures and reactions.

"Yes," she said, "with a lot of the people who go to these things, they can already do it. A workshop is an affirmation that what they are doing is correct. They hope that they may also learn a different way of doing it that would make the communication more powerful."

"These seem like support groups," I said to Denise. "During intermissions they tell each other stories about their animals."

"Sure," Denise said. "You can't sit down with your neighbor and say, my dog told me this. The men with the white suits would come for you. Most people won't publicly talk about this. When I started being more public about what I do, there was concern that I was doing voodoo or black magic or witchcraft, until people understood. I sometimes do volunteer teaching in the local school system's science programs. I have a degree in zoology. One time a boy had an asthma attack, and I used Reiki to pull him out of it. This frightened some people, but after I explained it and offered classes, people became intrigued, and are beginning to be more involved with alternative medicine. I answer questions openly and joke about it openly, and that relieves a lot of tension and stress and fear."

Carol Gurney of Agoura, California, is one of the most widely known teachers of animal communication. She has taught more than one thousand people over the past nine years. Although she is an admirer of Penelope Smith, she feels that her own method might be more geared to people who have had practically no experience with telepathic communication, who are complete beginners. She teaches a basic one-day workshop, at her home, and all over the country.

"Everybody who has taken the introductory workshop has gotten it and experienced the animals' telepathy," she told me. "People can learn animal communication in one day. I have not had anyone leave without having an experience that was validated for them. It's really up to them what they want to do with it. It's like going to your first French class. You can't expect to communicate fluently after your first class. It begins to open the doors, and you have the tools. Depending on the level to which you want to go, you need to practice to become fluent. I also have a more advanced training program, one weekend per month for four months."

Carol described the pattern of her introductory workshop as follows:

First, we talk about telepathy, how animals communicate to us telepathically, how we can communicate better telepathically to them. How we can enhance our relationships with animals, different techniques that are out there. Insights I have gained from animals, the things that they have taught me. Case histories of telepathic communication.

Once we've covered the basics, then we'll do a series of exercises. The first one is to get them to relax their minds and their bodies, and how to quiet their minds, because that's *the* most challenging thing for all of us humans to do. Then we have an exercise on how to send and receive information.

Then we have an exercise on how to communicate with each other through the use of color. I developed this exercise years ago, and wrote an article for Penelope Smith's paper, *Species Link*. Penelope liked the exercise so much that she asked if she could use it in her workshops, and also teach it to other instructors. So I imagine everybody is now doing this exercise in their workshops. The person sending the information would feel the color orange. I would ask the receivers, what did it feel like—was it soft, was it cool, is it bright, is it wet, is it damp? What is the tone of the color—is it bright or dull, dark or light orange? Did they observe any images or thoughts to muster up the color orange? So what they are doing is telepathically communicating on a feeling level and on a visual level and on a thinking level. They are sending their thoughts, feelings, and images.

After a break, the group will start communicating with one animal at a time, and we'll get validations as we go along. Some people will connect with one animal versus another.

Carol noted that there are various ways of communicating telepathically with animals—through words, feelings, or visualization. "Some teachers emphasize visualization," she said. "They'll say, 'If you ask your dog what his favorite meal is, send a mental image of his bowl, empty.' It's like a slide show. Then you wait to see what the bowl gets filled up with."

Carol shared more of her theories with me:

You can also use Gestalt, a psychotherapeutic technique. You become the person or animal. If you were having trouble with your spouse, the therapist would ask you to pretend that person is in the room, sitting in a chair. You tell the person how you feel. Then the therapist would ask you to sit in that seat, and he'd ask you how you feel. You pretend that you are becoming that person. You see and feel things through their eyes and emotions. It is unbelievable, the power of that communication. So I adopted that technique with animals. Say, for instance, a person is having a lot of difficulty in getting quiet and getting out of his own way. A good technique for them might be to ask a question of the animal and then pretend that they become that animal. Then they can give up being themselves and really see things as that animal sees things.

The technique that I use I call communicating from the heart. I direct my students through a guided meditation, the purpose of which is to get them in touch with that place within themselves, within their hearts, where all their compassion and love lives, so that what we can begin to do is communicate from our hearts, versus our minds. Because that's a big difference from if we communicate just from our minds. If we can move down into our heart center it comes through all of us. It comes through our minds, our hearts, our spirit, and our physical body. We come from pure love. If you do this you allow yourself and that animal to share information on all different levels. The animal will feel so safe with you that it begins to reveal to you things that it needs to.

One can do this sort of thing with people. And we do these exercises with people before we do it with animals. I've had lots of therapists in my workshops and they say, "Carol, I took this and I didn't know why I was taking it. I don't plan to do this professionally with animals. But it has helped me so much with my clients, because now I can telepathically listen to them and really know what's going on."

I mentioned to Carol that, being a New Agenik, I keep hearing about a change in consciousness that is impending—an awakening. I asked her, "Is communicating with animals part of this cosmic change that's going on?"

Carol Gurney

"I think so," she replied. "People are awakening, people want to know who their animals really are. The bottom line is that they want to know who *they* themselves are. Because animals are a reflection of us. One of the primary reasons for animals being in our lives is to teach us how to love ourselves the way they love us. They teach us through their behavior, through their actions, all about ourselves. They're our greatest mirrors, they're the greatest therapists we have on this earth."

8

A Funny Thing Happened on the Way to Communicating

As the reader may have noticed, this is a rather inclusive book. Its entirety ranges all over the North American continent, and into a few neighboring dimensions. It involves interviews with or observations of numerous people, dogs, cats, horses, llamas, and other fauna, as well as a variety of flora.

At this point I thought it might be a good idea to give the reader, and myself, a break—to toss in a few easy-to-read, easy-to-write anecdotes that don't seem to fit into my other chapters. But it's material that seemed to me too fascinating, astonishing, exciting, arcane, and charming to leave out of the book. Stories range from a constipated dog who knew the cure to a performing pig who was a real trouper.

During one of several interviews I had with Jeri Ryan, a leading animal communicator, she mentioned crossing paths with a constipated dog. He knew the cure too.

"I asked him what would help him," Jeri said, "and he said grated carrots. I thought, Oh boy, where does this come from? So I told his

Jeri Ryan with Ryan Patrick O'Ryan

person, he said grated carrots. So she gave him grated carrots and he stopped being constipated. Now he eats grated carrots all the time."

I asked Jeri if she thought a spirit guide might have slipped this helpful hint to the dog.

"I didn't ask him," she replied. "It might be. When the information comes in, I don't know where it comes from. I know it comes from the animal, but I don't know where the animal gets it. There's always the possibility that the animal has heard people talk about such things."

"I think I'll stash this away for the next time I get constipated," I said.

"I've thought about that, too," Jeri replied.

A couple of decades ago, I had a wonderful Irish setter named Seyde, who was extraordinarily beautiful even for her gorgeous breed. I would get home from work in the afternoon, go upstairs to my den, plop down in a lay-back chair, and prepare to meditate, or more likely, nap. Seyde would take up a sitting position on the floor beside the chair, and would pant, murmur, and make sounds that said in no uncertain way, "C'mon, let's go for a walk." I wouldn't be ready for a walk at that point, and would stolidly ignore her.

Lying back, searching for the alpha state, I would hear her mutters, sotto voce wails, laments, whines. I could stand it about two and a half minutes. Then I would think, Maybe I ought to take her for a walk.

Instantly, before I could open my eyes, I would hear Seyde flying down the stairs, stationing herself by the front door, making happy Ha-Ha-Ha noises. We would go through this act every afternoon.

I began to wonder how she would get such a fast start. I checked to see if my expression was changing. No, I seemed to be maintaining a poker face. I would surreptitiously open my eyes in a narrow squint, to see if I was moving ever so slightly. No, as far as I could tell, I was as immobile as a corpse.

I used to joke that Seyde could read my mind. Now I think that I wasn't kidding—she was doing just that.

I have a friend named Eugenia Macer-Story who lives in New York and is a talented psychic, poet, and playwright. (Her plays are slightly offbeat. A friend and I once appeared in one of them, playing the rear end of a dragon.) When I was doing research for this book, I called Eugenia to see what she had to say about animal communication. She always comes up with something interesting.

"When I was about five," she told me, "we were living in Texas. One day I went over to see some children friends I had in the neighborhood. They had a big dalmatian who was very friendly. When I got to their house I started walking up the driveway. The dog appeared and came toward me. He blocked me. He sort of herded me. He didn't growl, but every time I would move to go around him he'd move so that I couldn't get by him and enter the property. I petted him, but he was bigger than

Eugenia Macer-Story

me and he would not allow me to go up to the house. I finally gave up and went home.

"Later in the day, it was found that the man of the house had flipped out. He had a gun and had barricaded himself in the house, threatening to shoot his family and anybody else who came in. Actually, he was disarmed before he could hurt anyone. The dog had kept me from going up the driveway and into danger."

When I asked animal communicator Anita Curtis how she began communicating with animals, this is what she told me:

When I went to learn how to do it, I found out that I had been doing it for years and that there was a name for it. When I was young, there was one horse I could talk to. He could tell me what was going to happen, when he was going to be sick, when he was going to have an attack with his eyes, a lot of things that were going to happen to him. He was very accurate, but I thought it was just the one horse who could tell me these things.

A good many years later, I heard on TV about someone who had a dog who could do these miraculous tricks. The woman said she had trained it mentally with pictures. Soon after that, somebody told me that Jeri Ryan was going to be in Virginia teaching animal communication, and did I want to go? Boy, did I!

I took Jeri's workshop, and soon after I was going down to clean the stables, and I saw the horses walking toward the barn. I didn't want them to go in the door, because they'd stand on what I wanted to clean. So I pictured them standing outside, and when I looked again they were standing outside. I thought that was pretty neat, but I thought it must be a coincidence. So I pictured one horse walking in a circle and looking in the doorway. And when he did it, I figured that must be another coincidence. So I pictured he'd do it again. I figured he wouldn't do it again because he had already looked in. And he did it again! So I realized that I was getting on to it. Then I had him walk in circles, take three steps to the right, take three steps to the left. I drove the poor horse nuts.

I went down to the barn, where he was standing with the pony behind him. I wanted him to touch my face with his nose. And he just wouldn't do it. Maybe he was mad at me for putting him through all those paces. We were staring at each other, staring into each other's eyes, and I was sending these pictures. Finally the pony walked around him and touched my face with her nose. She looked the horse straight in the eye as though to say, "What are you, stupid or something?"

———

At the workshop I attended at Dawn Hayman's animal shelter, Dawn told us one of the saddest racehorse stories I've ever heard. At least it was sad for the horse's owner. Dawn said she was called in to evaluate a young horse, Gypsy, who had won very big on her first outing, but had never won a race since. Dawn had a chat with Gypsy and was able to pinpoint the problem. Gypsy said she hated to have other horses running behind her.

———

In the next chapter, you will find a story involving potbelly pigs. Unlike most people, I have a favorable impression of pigs, so I was eager to write about them and help improve their public image.

This soft spot for pigs in my memory bank dates from a newspaper story I wrote many years ago as a young reporter. One bitter winter day, I journeyed to a farm in Upstate New York to interview a man who, I was informed, had a "pig act." He did, indeed. He had trained half a dozen pigs, and had toured most of the available continents with them. In the winter, he and the pigs often rusticated on his brother's farm. The brother, I noticed, was not too respectful of the pig impresario.

"Tell him about the time you got stranded in South America and had to eat your act," he urged.

"Pay no attention to him," my interviewee said. "He's always been jealous of my career."

The pig entrepreneur gave me an entirely new slant on pigs. According to him, pigs were the most intelligent, loving, conscientious creatures on the face of the planet—way ahead of human beings, which isn't too hard to believe. Pigs are actually very clean, he insisted, it was just living with humans that forced them to become somewhat soiled.

I still remember the rousing climax of the act. The pigs would climb a sort of playground slide and slide down, one after another, over and over—zoom, zoom, zoom! It was quite spectacular. My most riveting memory came when one huge pig fell off the top of the slide and landed with a crash that must have been heard in Albany, thirty miles away. But he was so conscientious! He tottered around, groggy, almost out of it, but obviously mortified at having loused up the act. He immediately staggered back to the slide, climbed up it, and slid down again. The show must go on! I knew then that pigs are great.

The memory of that afternoon and that heroic pig may have influenced a response I gave a few months ago on a computer on-line program. I had been asked by a New York advertising company to be the answer man on a call-in show concerning ghosts, since I had written some books on the subject. I had done this sort of promotion on radio and TV, but on-line was new to me, so I thought it would be fun, and might even sell a book or two.

Somewhere along the way, one of the respondents asked if I was writing another book on ghosts and I said no, I was doing one about talking to animals, and hearing them talk back. One thing led to another, and pretty soon I was telling the agog audience that communicators kept telling me that animals reincarnated, and not only that, some human beings have been animals in past lives, and maybe will be again.

Across the screen came a question: DO YOU BELIEVE THAT GOING FROM BEING A HUMAN TO BEING AN ANIMAL IS A PUNISHMENT? I replied: NO, I THINK IT'S A PROMOTION.

The lady from the ad company who was in charge of the program called me up the next day to thank me and said that she thought my comment on going from human to animal was the high point of the show. She said she had considered flashing her own message on the screen—such as CHORTLE, CHORTLE, CHORTLE! or maybe RIGHT ON!—but didn't because she felt that in her position she ought to be neutral.

A friend of mine named Velsa Watterson often speaks of one of her best friends, a goose named Herman. "We've had a close association for ten years," she says. "I inherited him from my uncle."

Herman is thirty-five, which surprised me. I didn't know geese lived that long.

Velsa thinks it's because she has him on a healthy diet. "I buy only organic vegetables for Herman," she told me, "except for now and then a little lettuce I get from a restaurant. I think animals can live longer if they eat right—humans too."

I asked Velsa what kind of goose Herman was. "A white goose," she said. "I really don't know what kind of goose. He's just a beautiful goose, that's all."

She once gave me an interesting account of an adventure she had with Herman. She had heard a noise in her garage. On investigation, she found that a female cardinal had flown in and was having a rough time getting out. It was flying against a window, fluttering about in a panic. Velsa went over to the window and tried to encourage the little bird to fly out the door, but she got no response. She tried to gather it up so she could take it outside and free it. The bird did not cooperate; it was terrified, in a frenzy. Velsa decided to enlist the aid of Herman.

Herman had once helped when a groundhog was frightened of Velsa. He seemed to have gotten across the message to the groundhog that Velsa was OK, that she had only good intentions. Herman was outside in the backyard, so Velsa went to him.

"I put my arms around him," she told me, "and I said, 'There's a little bird inside the garage and she's frightened. You tell her not to be frightened, so I can bring her out.' Herman waddled to the entrance of the garage and stood there. I went in and said in my mind to the little bird, who was still flying against the window, 'You're OK,' and I put my hands right under her, and she settled down and stood quietly on my hands. I took her outside and released her in my mind, and she flew away, up into a tree."

I asked Velsa if she felt that Herman had said something reassuring to the bird. "I'm not sure who did what," she replied. "It was like a joining of the three of us. I knew, and the goose knew, and the little bird knew that everything was OK. After I had talked with Herman, I knew that things were going to be different. So I went into the garage with a different attitude. I knew this time the bird was not going to be afraid. It was like the three of us were one in purpose."

Jim Worsley

Jim Worsley, a communicator based in Richmond, Virginia, had an interesting talent as a child. He could find things. In fact, he still can, but now he knows how he does it.

"As a kid," Jim told me, "I was always given credit for finding lost articles, small things like watches or earrings, things like that. Later, when I was an adult, I realized that some of my pets were picturing to me where the things were, and I'd go find them. But I wasn't realizing it at the time."

When Jim grew up, he became a high school band director. Then he had an experience in rebirthing, which so impressed him that he became a professional rebirther. Rebirthing, according to Jim, makes people more aware of the things that are happening to them, what they are doing.

Jim was close to animals from early in his life. "I didn't have the happiest childhood," he told me. "We had a dog and a cat and I would sit out in the yard and tell them all my problems. What I know now is that they were just spending time with me while I talked it all out. At that time, I didn't know that I could receive messages back. But I realized later, probably as a result of my rebirthing experience, that the animals would be different when I was being attentive to them, and I could listen in the same way and hear what they were saying about things, or about themselves."

Jim says that the first time he was aware that he had asked an animal where something was located it involved something the animal itself had lost. "I had a dog that hurt herself and had to wear a big plastic collar. It's one of those things you rent from a veterinarian hospital, a quite expensive item. The first time the dog went out she came home immediately without it. This was the first time I realized I had asked where the thing was, and I just walked directly out to the fence, right to it, about one hundred yards away."

I awoke recently with a case of 1:00 A.M. insomnia, and turned on the television. There, on Conan O'Brien's late night talk show, was an attractive woman who looked familiar. I realized it was Dr. Joyce Brothers, with whom I'd had some contact in the 1960s, when I wrote a magazine article about her. She still looks very good.

Thirty years ago, before I met her, Joyce had impressed me as being stiff and solemn, at least in her public appearances. I was surprised to find that in person she was very witty and full of fun. Perhaps with all these years in the public eye she has become more at ease onstage. At any rate, with Conan she was providing something rare on the tube—intelligent, civilized, very funny banter.

Joyce began telling about a visit to the zoo. Two gorillas had begun to mate. The human mothers swooped up their kids and raced them off to the aviary or somewhere. I figured that Joyce was going to segue into how you shouldn't try to shield the kids from sex, they might as well get it right, and that what the gorillas were doing was educational. But Joyce wasn't about to editorialize, she just went on to describe what happened during that episode of passion at the zoo.

The gorillas mated face-to-face, Joyce reported. I wasn't clear on whether they were using the missionary position, she didn't get into that much detail, but it was interesting. She and Conan got to talking about sex cues. Joyce reported that the female gorilla had grabbed the male by his foot. That seemed to get things started. This led to a discussion about human sex cues. Joyce suggested that the most unmistakable sex cue on the part of a human female is when the woman takes off her clothes.

She went on to remark that the gorillas' encounter was very quick. Conan protested that Joyce shouldn't have said that, it was unfair to the boy gorilla to reveal his lack of sophisticated sexual expertise to a nationwide audience. It could, Conan said, lead to a lifelong emotional trauma on the part of the boy gorilla if he found out that his gaucherie had been exposed publicly, even though this wasn't prime time.

In any case, I felt that Joyce's and Conan's interchange had been something of a landmark on late night television—something not dumb, something funny.

Animal communicators are asked to communicate all sorts of messages to animals. A case in point is Spudders, a Canadian cat. He is part of the family of Brenda and John Colebrooke of British Columbia, whom we met in Chapter 6. The communicator involved is Sharon Lunde.

Brenda told me that Spudders would lie on people's faces at night when they were asleep. This was a very friendly routine he had, but Brenda was afraid that somebody—particularly one of the kids—might get smothered.

"We asked Sharon to communicate with Spudders," Brenda said, "and ask him why he did this. He said that he felt that his role here was to be very close to us at night, to protect us from—as he said—night spirits. Sharon helped him work through this fear for us. She explained our problem with this, and he has never since tried to lie on our faces. Now you'll awaken and you'll be cheek to cheek with whiskers—but he's not on your face."

And then there was the man who went into a movie theater and realized, as his eyes became accustomed to the darkness, that a dog was occupying the seat in front of him. The dog was sitting straight up, watching the screen intently. A woman was sitting beside him. After a few minutes, the man leaned over and tapped the woman on the shoulder.

"Excuse me, ma'am," he said, "but I couldn't help admiring your dog's intelligence. He hasn't taken his eyes off the screen for a moment."

"I know," said the woman, "it's surprising to me too. He hated the book."

9

When Your Beloved Animal Dies

Teresa Wagner, an animal communicator based in Monterey, California, characterizes herself as "specializing in issues surrounding euthanasia, death, loss, and grief." She has a master's degree in counseling, and gives workshops on grieving and the loss of animals.

"The death of a being we love is such a poignant experience," she says. "I feel that people who lose their animals—who lose anyone who means a great deal to them, of course—need and deserve a tremendous amount of empathy from other beings around them. There's no such thing as skipping the emotional part, and it can be a wonderful opportunity for growth. When someone in our life whom we value deeply dies there's always an opportunity for transformation, because that someone who was a part of who we are is no longer in that form. And that gives us a chance to do all kinds of things.

"Early literature on grief talks a lot about getting things back to the way they were. Depending on the particular loss, that can be all right. But the new thinking is that when we feel grief we can do a lot more than just cope. I feel you can go beyond mere coping and really grow, even transform, as a result of your loss."

Teresa began practicing professionally as an animal communicator at the suggestion of Jeri Ryan, with whom she had trained. She had already done a considerable amount of work in the field of grief, some of it with people who had lost or were in the process of losing their animals.

Armed with a counseling background from her mainstream education, she moved into the esoteric field of animal communication from a most conventional one, the corporate life. After graduate study in counseling at Villanova University, in Pennsylvania, she worked for RCA in New York as a training and development manager, working her way up the corporate ladder.

"Halfway through my RCA career," she relates, "I lost my first cat as an adult. I grieved deeply. I couldn't get over it. I saw a therapist and read a lot about grief. A veterinarian I knew urged me to do grief work, and to conduct support groups for people who had lost animals. In 1989 I started a practice with animals. I still also do management consulting for corporations. I also do grief workshops involving animals. I work with people who have lost their animals, and often with workers in animal shelters, people who have to perform euthanasia over and over again. The stress these people who work in shelters undergo, their grief, is tremendous."

Like many communicators, and indeed a good number of ordinary animal lovers, Teresa had a difficult childhood. "Luckily," she says, "I came into this lifetime with a gift and a comfort in connection with the animal kingdom. That was very, very strong early on. My mother says I would cry and cry if she took me to the zoo, I pitied the animals so much. I came into this life to learn certain lessons and finish karmic things, but the buffer for me, the sweetness and softness from the very beginning, has been the animals.

"There are a lot of people out there—bereaved owners and animal shelter people—who have had experiences similar to mine. Their intense connection to animals is sometimes—although not in every case—connected to early experiences of trusting animals more than people. Although I think it's very important for us who are so connected to animals to continue our own healing with humans."

The story of Cal, a feral cat, and Sheila, her person, is an example of the way Teresa is called upon to soften crises and grief. (A feral animal is a wild animal. There are a lot of feral cats around.)

"Cal was extremely hostile," Teresa relates. "Feral cats live outside, they never had a home. They look just like house cats, but they have never lived with people. Most of these cats want to remain wild, they have a very different temperament from a house cat. They look the same, but many of them are terrified at the thought of living within the boundaries of a home. It's like dealing with a little bobcat.

"There are people all over the country who care about feral cats. They feel sorry for them. Cal was part of a feral colony, and Sheila took care of these cats. She fed them; she knew every cat. She took pictures of them, and if one was missing she knew it.

"Cal wasn't around for awhile. Finally Sheila was able to find her and catch her and take her to a vet, who found that she was having a life-threatening illness. What should they do, what would be best for Cal? Did Cal want to be released and die naturally in the colony, or did she want help in dying?"

Sheila and the vet called on Teresa to communicate with Cal, to try to find out what Cal wanted.

"One of the really helpful, practical things in animal communication," Teresa said, "can come when a person knows their animal is dying from a disease or accident, and the person must make a choice. They can help the animal die through euthanasia or let it die naturally. That's a very big responsibility."

People agonize over this dilemma. It involves love, grief, guilt—a whole range of difficult, painful emotions. Teresa's communication with Cal alleviated much of the distress of the situation for all concerned.

"When we talked to Cal," Teresa says, "and let her know what was happening, Cal said, 'Yes, I want help in dying.' The vet was stunned to see this feral cat, who usually acted so wild—biting, screaming, and scratching—just lie in his arms and accept the needle.

"The most moving part of this were the messages that Cal had for Sheila," Teresa relates. "She said such wonderful things about Sheila, how the cats loved her and appreciated the things she did for them. It was a love that went far beyond their gratitude for the food she brought them every day."

———

Death for an animal, according to the several dozen animal communicators I have spoken with, is not as onerous as it may be for a human being. Phil Roberts, the former New Hampshire dairy farmer, told me,

"I can honestly tell people that it's no big deal to the animal to be put down. There is absolutely no sense of death. They can remember their past lives. They know there's going to be a future life. They can teach us about life and death, birth, and dying.

"If an animal is in pain, it can travel in its mind to a comfortable place. What we humans do, with modern medicine, is not extend life, but prolong death."

Phil, like most of the other animal communicators I talked with, told me he often speaks with animals who have died, who are in spirit.

I might interject that these people—these communicators—are well-educated, intelligent folk, people that an experienced investigative reporter like myself tends to believe. They strike me as people who not only have all their marbles, but know where all those marbles are, which I feel is more than can be said for most of us. In other words, they have mastered aspects of their unconscious mind that most of us are unaware of, at this stage of human awareness.

"You can tell," Phil said, "if the animal you are talking to (at a distance) is alive or dead. It just feels different. I recently spoke with a horse that had been taken to a veterinary hospital. Everybody had decided that the horse should be put down. I talked to her at night and she had not been put down. I talked with her the next day and she had been. It was almost glorious after she had been. There was no pain, and she was happy. She was worried about how her people were doing. She didn't want her people to grieve."

Winterhawk, the California communicator who changed her name from Liz, told me, "I like most to assist people when it's time for their animals to leave their body. That's a tender and tough time. A lot of times the animals are not ready to leave their bodies; they just need a different kind of intervention, such as chiropractic or something. The animals can answer any questions that you'd like them to field, like a person could. They give their opinions."

Sometimes, according to Winterhawk, these opinions are strikingly valid. She tells of a horse that had become very difficult. Its owner, a woman, had been thrown by the horse. The horse had become very hostile, attempting to bite anyone who came near him.

"This was very much out of character for this horse," Winterhawk related. "The vet couldn't find anything wrong with him. They were going to put him to sleep. But I had a feeling he was not seriously sick, and that he didn't want to die. I checked in with the horse. He said his back hurt so much that he could not stand to have a rider, and that was why he had thrown his owner. I suggested that the woman contact a certain chiropractor, and within one treatment the horse was all right, no longer in pain."

Another communicator with an offbeat name calls herself Sananjaleen. She lives in Rectortown, Virginia, and speaks with a clipped English accent. I asked her where this intriguing name comes from and she laughed and gave me an eminently reasonable explanation.

"It came in meditation," she said. "I belong to a meditation group. We call these names our higher self—or angelic—names. My 3-D name, as I put it, is June Hughes. When we first get these names we get very excited about them, we get carried away. So I started using the name for my writings. I came over here in 1962. I was a horse person, always working with horses, and now I write about them."

Sananjaleen says she specializes in "words of comfort received from animals who have made the transition." She told me:

It just seemed to evolve that I can get these beautiful messages from the animals, and it relieves people's guilt. Some people have incredible guilt that they didn't do the right thing by the animal. And my messages seem to be getting deeper. Or perhaps they get deeper as I grow. Also, I wonder if the people who are drawn to me are the ones who can receive deeper messages. You don't know where the circle begins.

Ever since I was a little child I wanted to talk to the animals. But I think I put everything on hold because I was afraid of what I would hear. I was afraid that I would hear that they were unhappy. It wasn't till my own little dog, Gretel, a long-haired dachshund, died. I had learned to meditate, and I had read a lot of spiritual books. I started sending Gretel my love, and for the next three years she was teaching me. She would tell me different things she was doing. I'd tell my

Sananjaleen

friends and they'd want me to try to get information about their own dogs through Gretel. And then it just sort of evolved that I could do it without Gretel. As a child, I was not aware of having psychic abilities. It was the Gretel thing that got me going, which was fairly recently.

I now work almost entirely with animals that have died. When people phone in I take a few notes. I do it in my own meditation time. I call for the spirit of the animal to come.

For example, a woman wanted to know if her cat will ever come back to her again. And the cat said something like, "She will know the presence of my energy because I will play a tune upon her cells." Those words were particularly meaningful to the woman because, although I didn't know it at the time, she was a flutist.

Very often the animals give messages in words that are meaningful to their owners. Like a horse said something about helping his owner in her dance through life. The owner used to be a ballet dancer, which I hadn't known at the time.

One animal gave her owner a message that when things no longer flow and move easily maybe it's because they're complete, and it's time to go on to something else. The owner took this as a direct suggestion to stop trying to patch her job up, to quit and head off into an entirely different line of work.

I asked Sananjaleen if she believed that animals reincarnate. She replied, "Animals definitely reincarnate. Often when I call for an animal's spirit the message is that they are an emanation, or part of, a tiny piece of a great angel. Or quite often their person's higher self or master teacher. To say, my dog is an angel, well, people might have trouble with that idea, but when you say, this great angel sent a tiny piece of itself in the form of a cat or dog to bring you comfort and joy, then it's more understandable."

Often, the animal is in the caring position rather than the person, according to Sananjaleen. "People often feel great guilt when they put their animal asleep. They cannot bring themselves to do it. Sometimes the animal is lingering on to teach their person to take charge of his or her life, to teach them to make the decision. And more than once I've found that when the person has made the decision and called the vet, and when the vet is on the way there, the animal will die before the needle reaches it. The animal says, 'There, that's all they have to do, make the decision, and then I can go.'"

Sananjaleen provides another example of an animal's taking on the teaching role. It occurred, she relates, during an animal communication workshop she was giving in her home:

It happened to a woman I knew nothing about except that she had ten dogs, ten strays that she had taken in and given a home to. She was doing this little workshop exercise with us. She had my oldest dog, Tibby, in her arms. Tibby was a long-haired dachshund, fourteen years old. Tibby was asleep, with her head resting on the woman's chest. And in her mind, the woman told us, she heard Tibby say, "I have come to the end of my mission. I have almost completed my life, and I'm in good shape. But your cat has come to the end of his mission, and he is not in good shape. You must let him go."

And what none of us knew was that the woman had a fifteen-year-old cat who had cancer, and she was trying to decide whether to keep him alive or have him euthanized.

Do I believe all this? I maintain an open mind.

And I try to remember advice given me by a parapsychologist I interviewed when I wrote my first book on the occult, about fifteen years ago. He is Boyce Batey of Bloomfield, Connecticut, and he said, "In this whole field you walk a very narrow path between having an open mind and a hole in the head."

I mentioned in the Preface of this present book that my books on spirits—ghosts—are quite popular at the Massachusetts Institute of Technology, that world-class bastion of left-brain thinking. Many of the people I have been hanging out with the past twenty-five years—very right-brain spiritual types—sometimes suspect I am an analytical spy in their midst. I do try to straddle both worlds. It's enough to give one a hernia.

I am constantly trying to introduce the two opposite hemispheres of my brain to each other, so far without notable success. I study with various guru types—teachers of meditation, yoga, and other Eastern, New Age, and otherwise esoteric disciplines. Recently, I wrote an article about a young man named Alan Schultz, of Worcester, Massachusetts, one of my frustrated instructors. We hug trees and rocks together. They don't speak to me yet, but I'm hanging in there. I asked Alan what he thought of me as a client, and this was his reply:

You're the most resistive client I've ever had. Always sloughing off or undoing the healing work done. For the longest time I considered myself a failure because this guy was never making progress. You were trying for spiritual growth, but every step you'd take you'd take two backward. Whenever you'd get into unknown territory, you'd get intellectual about it. You'd say, "This can't be real," and you'd dissolve all the magic that had happened. We'd go around the universe in meditation, into other lifetimes, and you'd say, "I must have imagined it all. It might be true, but I don't know." You'd rationalize mystic events to death, till they weren't real anymore.

You have to choose to believe you are a spirit in a body, not a mind in a body thinking about being a spirit. When you choose a different reality you'll be a more spiritual being. Then you'll grow like crazy, because you have so much information within you. You're a walking encyclopedia of spiritual information, but all you do is intellectually use that information. You need to keep logic from getting in the way of your intuition.

I *have* had one experience in which my beloved pet, Seyde, who had died, came into my awareness. She was a gorgeous Irish setter. I was married at the time, and we had Seyde and a cat. The cat's name was Pooka. When my wife and I parted, she got custody of Pooka and I got Seyde, although we each had visiting privileges. We lived in Pittsfield, in Berkshire County, the western edge of Massachusetts. On becoming single again, I rented a house in Lenox, six miles south, and took a post office box in Pittsfield. Every morning I would drive up to Pittsfield to get my mail. Seyde would accompany me.

Sometime later I moved to the Boston area. I joined a Spiritualist church to see what they were up to. Every so often they would have a Mediums' Day to help finance the church. Various mediums—usually members of the congregation—would be available for ten-minute readings.

One time on a Mediums' Day I chose a young man who later became a law student. This young man's name was Jim Apostle.

Jim began telling me there was the spirit of a dog present. He said that he could see me leaving a house, coming down the steps to a car. The dog would jump toward me repeatedly, pretending to bite my arms, putting her teeth lightly on the sleeve of my jacket. It was our game.

Then I would open the door of the car, and the dog's manner would change. She would daintily, sedately step into the car and sit on the front seat.

Jim then saw me getting behind the wheel and starting the car. When I had backed out of the driveway, and was driving along the road, I would reach over and stroke the dog's head. After a minute or two of that, the dog would initiate the next part of the game. She would flop over onto me, and lay her head on my chest. We would drive along for two or three minutes, and then this part of the game would end. The dog would get up and sit, in a very dignified manner, looking out the windows of the car and taking in the scenery.

Seyde and I had at one time done this every morning. And Jim described exactly the way it happened. Could he have been reading my mind? I certainly wasn't thinking of Seyde when the reading began. I like to think that Jim was really functioning as a medium, as a link to the next world, and that Seyde's spirit had come through and had reenacted our morning ritual in Lenox.

I was afraid to ask Jim what sort of dog he had seen. I didn't want to take a chance of spoiling the experience.

———————

Griffin Kanter of Houston, Texas, whom we have met before in these pages, told me:

I have often worked with animals who have died, and I especially enjoy that aspect of communication. I find it a wonderful personal blessing to be able to assist people at that time, at the end of their physical time together with their animals. It's a wonderful closure, it's usually a wonderful exchange of love, sharing stories from all the years they've been together.

Sometimes I'm not involved until the animal has already made the transition, and then we talk and the animal has the opportunity to talk from a different perspective, no longer being in the physical body, no longer being sick, no longer being old. Sometimes they talk about what their purpose was in that human's life.

I just talked with a woman whose dog was young, who didn't have a long-term illness. He was a small terrier who jumped out of the car, landed wrong and injured his back and had to be put down. The dog was talking about how its life was interrupted. That's how it felt. It hadn't adjusted itself. I talked to it about two weeks after it was put down, and it was still in that transition of adjusting to the energy instead of the physical.

He was a tiny little dog whose name was Rambo. I thought that was so cute. But he *was* a very strong personality, so in a way the name really fit. He said that he was able to help his person love in a way that she hadn't loved before. And his death, as unexpected as it was, allowed her to grieve over many things she had not allowed herself to grieve over before. She hadn't been able to communicate. Sometimes your own grief gets in the way.

What I suggest to people is to do dream work, to ask to be able to contact the animal in the dream state. We seem to be able to do things in the dream state that we can't do when we're conscious. And sometimes the animal is able to come, and you're able to remember the dream, and you're able to touch them and hold them and pet them again.

Rambo wanted his human to get another dog as soon as possible and not to wait, because he wanted her to have that kind of love. And he would come back as soon as he could. He wanted to come back, because he felt his life was interrupted. He would make sure he got back.

———————

Dawn Hayman tells a similar story about the remorse that can cluster around euthanasia. She told me:

One lady called me around Thanksgiving time and she wanted to talk to a horse who had died a few years before that she felt very guilty about. She had had to have him euthanized, and always wondered if she had done the right thing. I connected with the horse and the horse said, "Tell her I'm thinking about her a lot this week. Tell her I can still hear the bells."

I said this to the woman, who was very skeptical about my communicating with an animal who had passed away. She just started crying. I said, "I'm getting like sleigh bells." There was no way I could possibly have known this, but what she used to do was go trail riding, and when hunting season started, just around Thanksgiving, she would cover her saddle and the horse with giant sleigh bells and go riding through the woods. That would keep them safer from the hunters. She was well known around her neighborhood for that, you could hear them coming for miles.

Playing my usual skeptical, devil's advocate role, I asked Dawn if there was any possibility that she could have been pulling this out of the woman's mind.

"People have asked me that," Dawn replied. "I don't know. But the message from the horse meant a lot to the woman. I've had lots and lots of situations like that, where the animals have passed away and wanted their owners to know something important."

She assured me she was not offended by my question.

"I have an open mind," she said, "but I'm always the first one to be skeptical. You have to hit me over the head with something before I'll believe it."

Donetta Zimmerman, the Cincinnati communicator, told me it is not unusual for an ailing animal to be helped into the next world by an animal friend who has already gone on.

"I remember a husky dog who was comatose," she said. "I can't talk to an animal when it is sleeping, but the thought patterns are different when it is in a coma, and I am then able to communicate. This dog was saying, 'My friend's [his owner's] dog—the dog I grew up with—is coming back to get me. She's here now, she wants me to go with her, and I want to go with her. I want to go, but I can't because my owner will grieve so badly. She won't release me.'"

Donetta spoke with the woman, who told her, "I just can't bear to part with this dog."

Donetta urged the woman to talk with her vet as quickly as possible, and let the dog go, and she did.

Carol Wright, originally a student of Griffin Kanter, now practices animal communication in San Francisco. Carol had her first contact with Griffin when they both lived in Texas, and Griffin told her how to find a lost cat. Here's how Carol describes it:

My cat Lucy had gotten lost. I called up Griffin to see if she could help, and she told me how to bring her home, mentally. And she came home the next day. Actually, this started me with animal communication.

I had Griffin out to my house and she talked to all of the animals—I have several. I had a cat whose quality of life I was very concerned about. He was ill, and I wanted to make sure that I wasn't keeping him here. Griffin helped with that. She had me asking questions of the cat: Are you happy? Are you wanting to drop your body, or are you wanting to stay? How are you feeling overall? Is life still enjoyable?

His answers were yes, until the day I put him to sleep. It was obvious that he was in terrible distress, and he was ready. Griffin helped on the phone to confirm that with me, because I was of course very emotional. But the cat was ready. When I took him to the vet, he all but put out his little paw for the vet to inject. He was ready.

Carol took a brief workshop with Griffin, only a couple of hours. I was a bit startled that Carol got the hang of animal communication so easily.

"Basically," Carol explained, "Griffin just gave me permission to do something that I've always done, something I hadn't really thought about."

Carol is one of those lucky—or unlucky, depending on which side of the fence you're sitting—people who is a natural psychic.

"I don't remember ever not having that ability," she told me. "For example, I would know something was going to happen before it happened. I told my parents that my grandmother was ill, and the phone call came a few hours later. Stuff like that has always been there for me."

Carol, who is a nurse, said, "With animals, I don't know that it's being psychic so much as knowing that they can communicate. If you don't have blocks, they can speak pretty clearly."

I suggested, "I guess the thing is to be able to listen."

She replied emphatically, "Yeah!"

"This ability," she went on, "is not something you usually talk to people about, especially a few years ago in Houston, Texas. But Griffin gave me permission. I had always felt that I understood animals clearly, I just hadn't given myself permission to really acknowledge it."

Carol told me of helping a horse make a decision to leave this plane of existence.

"This woman," Carol said, "had this old horse named Buck who was having pretty bad arthritis. She pretty much felt that it was time for him to be put down, so I went out to talk to him about that. He very clearly stated that he didn't want anybody to put a hammer to his head, something I had never heard of. I didn't know they sometimes did that to horses. So they told him what they were going to do, and he asked for two more weeks because he wanted to tell all his friends and get closer to them. And then the vet came and gave him an injection."

Carol also told me some stories about potbelly pigs, a breed of God's creatures that I had never heard of, but who certainly sound fascinating. She told me how three pigs were able to give physical and emotional solace to another pig, who was in desperate straits after having been attacked by dogs. This account was given to me jointly by Carol and the keepers of the pigs, Marcy and Chris Christianson. Marcy surveys property for fire insurance; her husband Chris is a high school teacher. Marcy also works with the California Potbelly Pig Association. "We rescue pigs and find them good homes," she explained.

It was Carol who started me off on potbelly pigs.

"They're a lot of fun," she said. "They're very arrogant. Little Vietnamese potbelly pigs. They've kind of turned into a designer animal. They grow to about 150 pounds, but they're very cute, very intelligent. There's one I've worked with a lot. He's had a horrible leg problem. His name is T.S. He was named after T. S. Eliot."

I asked if T.S. wrote poetry, and Carol said, "He hasn't come up with poetry yet. I guess it just hasn't occurred to him. He's very grumpy and he's proud of it, and he's as opinionated as you can get. I guess you could call him pigheaded."

I got in touch with Marcy and she told me that T.S.'s name was not T. S. Eliot, even though he was named after the famed poet. His name was T. S. Pigliot. Marcy said she was very impressed when Carol was talking with one of the pigs and asked the pig about a dog he had known. The pig said, "He was OK for a dog with three legs."

"There was no way Carol could have known that the dog had only three legs," Marcy told me. "That was the beginning of our association with Carol."

Marcy also told me she had put toys and dolls in T.S.'s pen to keep him occupied. "He got very involved in the TV coverage of the O. J.

Simpson trial," Marcy said. "I could tell because he would wag his tail when it came on. Potbelly pigs have straight tails, and they wag them like a dog when they are pleased. When the O.J. trial would come on, T.S. would start wagging his tail. If it went into a lunch break or a commercial, he'd stop. He's a very smart pig.

"One day Chris gave him a pillow to put his head on. The very first thing he told Carol that night was, 'Thank Daddy for the pillow.' There's no way she could have known about that pillow except from the pig's mind."

Marcy told me that Carol had also worked with a pig who had spina bifida. His name was Sheriff of Rottingham. "We had him at the UC–Davis veterinary school," Marcy said. "They had x-rayed his front legs. When Carol talked to the Sheriff he told her he thought they should x-ray his rear legs, and she passed this on to Chris and me."

But it was the case of Timothy that completely convinced the Christiansons of Carol's psychic ability. "We're both skeptics," Marcy told me, "but with Timothy we became true believers."

Carol and Marcy had been talking on the telephone when the operator cut in to tell Marcy there was an emergency.

"I told Marcy to take the call," Carol told me, "and before I could hang up the phone I was assaulted by this terrible pain. I couldn't even reach to hang up the phone. I got this image of a little pig having horrible pain, and bleeding."

Marcy told me that there was no way that Carol could have heard the operator when she came on with the message about the pig.

"I called Marcy back in about an hour," Carol told me, "and found that this pig had been assaulted by two rottweilers and had been badly torn up. His name was Timothy, he told me his name. They ended up taking him to UC–Davis, and they euthanized him the next day. But he became very calm once they had rescued him, because I was talking with him. He just absolutely popped into my consciousness out of nowhere."

The most extraordinary aspect of this account involves the way three others of the Christiansons' pigs helped Timothy with his pain. Marcy told me, "These three pigs—T.S., the Sheriff, and a pig we call Chuckles—were helping Timothy psychically to get out of his pain. During the hours before Timothy was euthanized, Carol said these pigs were with him the whole time, although they were at home, seventy miles away from where Timothy was. They helped him to release from this life and go on. He was calm and peaceful at the end."

———————

Adele Tate is an animal communicator who lives in Byron, Illinois, about ninety miles northwest of Chicago. She is very much involved with spiritual awareness, as distinct from conventional religion.

"I talk to trees and streams," she told me. "I think of that as spiritual awareness. It certainly has to do with being able to see what is beyond the physical.

"Reincarnation is a foundation of my belief system. It's hard to comfort people about their animals if they don't know that animals come back over and over within the same person's lifetime. I've seen several examples of that.

"I've been surrounded by much hysteria recently. People say, 'You're psychic.' They see that as bad. There is a great fear right now in the religious arena."

Adele manages an air traffic control facility for the Federal Aviation Administration. Her husband teaches eighth grade language arts, drama, and volleyball.

"He is very sympathetic with what I do," Adele says. "I asked him this morning if he thinks the animal work I do is black magic, and he laughed. 'No,' he said, 'it's something that everybody can do, but we forgot.'"

Adele told me a moving story about the death of Windstan, a quarter horse in Iowa:

His person, Susan, called me and said Windstan's feet were very bad. He had what they call navicular disease. It's very painful. It's a disease of the navicular bone, in his case in his front feet. The bone deteriorates. So what they do is remove the nerve in the leg. Windstan had been nerved, and he was still very crippled, so she couldn't ride him. But she loved the horse. He was a soul mate of hers, and he was a very wise being.

Anyway, Susan called me to ask if Windstan wanted to be put down. She was afraid that he did, she was afraid that he didn't. There was a lot of emotion involved. I wanted to make sure that I was doing what was right for everybody. I spent a lot of time talking with him. He wanted me to write Susan a letter. He dictated a letter to her about his death, about his life.

Windstan told me a lot about Susan and the things they have done together, and she verified those things. He also told me that he wanted his children to be there when he died. He wanted to be euthanized. I asked him when he wanted to do this. He told me the phase of the moon, and he said that his life would end at "the beginning of the end and the end of the beginning."

Susan was very worried about whether she should have his body removed, or she should bury it, or what. She went round and round about that.

It finally happened on a Monday. That morning a young man called. He was maybe seventeen years old. He had known this horse since he was a child. His father had trained Windstan at one time. Windstan was a great roping horse. He had worked with cattle. He had done just about everything that a horse can do, and everybody knew him for miles around. Everybody knew who Windstan was. He was very famous out there.

This boy called Susan and asked to be there, and he brought a young friend. They were both working cowboys. They came out with their belt buckles and their boots and their hats. They had braided a necklace of alfalfa hay, and they put it around Windstan's neck.

Susan said, "What if he gets upset when I open up the barn door and he sees the big hole that has been dug to bury him in? What if he runs away? I don't want to be chasing him around. What if he doesn't indicate that he wants to go?"

I said I didn't think she'd have to worry about that, because he does want to go, and this is the day. So when she opened the barn door he walked purposefully right to the edge of the hole. They had dug it into the side of a hill, so that his body wouldn't exactly drop in. She said she hadn't wanted his body to be moved after it dropped to the ground.

Windstan had told me that he didn't want to be buried in his leather halter, that it was very expensive. Susan had laughed when I told her that. She told me she had had him in this barn where everybody had these very expensive leather halters for their horses. She didn't want Windstan to be thought of as a lesser class than the others, so she went out and bought him this $125 halter. He said to save it for when he comes back. So she had gone out and bought him a white nylon halter that was much less expensive—it was just a rope—and that's what he was buried in.

He died at a time between the full moon and a new moon. That's when I realized what he meant by "the end of the beginning and the beginning of the end."

I asked Adele if Windstan has come back, and she replied, "He had chosen his mother, and Susan had that horse. He had wanted to come back right away, but things didn't work out as far as getting the right father. But Susan thinks he may have been incarnated in another horse out there that lives very close by."

I asked Adele what her parents thought of her psychic abilities, and this is the answer she gave me:

My parents had a hard time with it, because they're westerners. Both were raised on farms, where animals are commodities. My dad thinks horses are for work. When I wrote them explaining what I was doing, my dad called and said, "I hope you're not quitting your full-time job." He would make fun of me a little bit.

Then one time he called and said he had been talking to a man who does a lot of meditating. He respects this man's opinions. And he told the man that his daughter talks to animals. And the man started listening intently. And my dad told him some of the stories that show there is some communicating going on. I had told these stories to my dad. And while my dad was telling him a story about a dog in Florida, the man started crying. And my dad said, "Why are you crying?"

And the man said, "You should never make fun of your daughter. She's got a gift of God, a very, very precious gift. You should not be making fun of that."

So my dad called to tell me he is not ever going to make fun of me again about it.

10

Do Animals Reincarnate?

D o animals reincarnate—do they have many lives? Almost every animal communicator of whom I asked that question answered yes. With almost complete unanimity, communicators told me that past lives could be seen in the animals' minds, if the animals chose to show them, and many did, if asked.

The first animal communicator I interviewed while researching this book sprung this idea on me. He was a seemingly quite serious, level-headed young man, with a scientific education. His name was Sean Ebnet. I had started work on the book on April Fool's Day. Could Ebnet be joking, I wondered for a split moment. But he stuck to his story, and practically everybody I've asked since has come up with the same answer.

Early in my research, I interviewed Teresa Wagner, who specializes in working with people who have been plunged into grief over an animal's death. I asked her if she believes that animals reincarnate, and she replied, "Absolutely, they come back. Reincarnation is laughable when you first hear it, but I've heard it so many times from the animals."

When Teresa trained to be an animal communicator, she studied with two of the leading luminaries in the field, Penelope Smith and Jeri Ryan. "You'll hear this from them too," Teresa told me.

When I queried Penelope on the subject, she sent me her book, *Animals . . . Our Return to Wholeness*, in which she devotes an entire chapter to animal reincarnation.

"Without exception," Teresa told me, "I have never talked to an animal in the process of dying, or who had already died, who was afraid of death. They know they have had past lives and will have future lives. They're very different from humans. I think most people are terrified of death because of their religious beliefs."

We humans seem to have blocked out so much information that our minds are potentially capable of registering.

Teresa also said that death, even a traumatic death, is not such an ordeal for animals, since they are able to withdraw their consciousness from their bodies. "Animals are usually not upset by death," Teresa said, "because they leave their bodies before there is any great emotional or physical trauma, even though the body might or might not be dead yet. Some coyote might be ripping their body apart, but there is no physical pain."

———

According to my informants, animals do not always come back in the same species. Dogs become horses, cats become dogs. Also—hold your hat—they purportedly sometimes come back as humans, or were human in past lives. The people who purport this challenging idea are animal communicators. I ran into this concept early on, and I kept on running into it.

Here is a relatively simple, easy-to-read, example—cat to horse. Adele Tate told it to Penelope Smith, and Penelope put it into her book.

A friend of Adele's named Sally had a horse named Dee, who, as Adele put it, was a "four-legged pogo stick when a human tried to board her." Adele spoke with Dee, and the horse wanted to know why her human couldn't walk beside her. "That would be more fun, wouldn't it?" suggested the horse.

So Adele asked Dee about past lives, and received a picture of a beautiful white cat, as she was in her previous life. Dee said her owner constantly left her to ride her horse. The cat was envious of the horse's close relationship with the person, and decided that next time around she'd try being a horse.

In an interview with me, Adele said that Dee had found that horses have to work pretty hard, and she wasn't too thrilled with that. She seemed unaware of her actual size, and couldn't understand why her person wanted to sit on her back.

"So she really wanted to be out of her horse body and go back to being a cat," Adele said. "But I talked her into sticking around and using that life and not wasting it, to try to get as much out of the experience as she could."

———

Phil Roberts, the former New Hampshire dairy farmer, was one of my early interviewees, and introduced me to some of these concepts. I keep coming back to Phil because I can't conceive of a dairy farmer as being anything other than clean-cut and down-to-earth. It's not as though he was a writer who's lived in perverse places like Boston or New York. I'll provide here two excerpts from one of our interviews. I'll start with the easier idea to assimilate into one's belief system.

"A husky told me," Phil said, "that he had always been a working dog in other lives. And now he was a pet. He wanted to work, and this caused a problem. He wanted to be in harness, he wanted to pull a sled."

Skeptics in the audience are probably thinking, that's just instinct, that's just common sense. Although other skeptics might be musing that common sense is a contradiction in terms.

Now try *this* idea from Phil:

I talked with a tiny little terrier at the animal shelter in Camden. His owner was there. It turned out that these two, the woman and the dog, had always been together. Once it was as a mother and daughter. Sometimes one would be the dog and the other would be the person. Sometimes they'd both be people. But they were a pair.

I made some gently skeptical noises, but he said he felt this principle to be absolutely true.

"They say we tend to exist in groups," Phil said. "We meet the same spirits in many lives."

———

Another of my early interviewees, Nedda Wittels, buttressed this concept. Nedda is a cultured woman, seemingly as sane as the rest of us, if not more so. She holds a bachelor's degree from Cornell, and master's degrees from New York University and the University of the State of New York at New Paltz. She taught public school, and then, before becoming a professional animal communicator, spent ten years in the computer world, specializing in software design and development. She grabbed my attention a bit when she said:

I believe in reincarnation. I know a bit about some of my own previous lives. One thing I know is that my horse Echo and I have been together many times before. Sometimes she was a horse, sometimes I was a horse. We've been together in a supportive, loving way many, many times. I think mostly she's been a horse; she likes being a horse.

Sharon Lunde, an animal communicator who lives in British Columbia, another of my convincingly sane-seeming interviewees, told me about her relationship with her horse, Bonn Jovi, and recited a poem she said the horse had composed. A *good* poem. I plan to devote a chapter to poetry by animals, but references to poetry keep slipping in prematurely. I asked Sharon how an animal could compose poetry. She told me:

That's very hard for people to grasp. For me it's easy, because animals come back again; they are reincarnated. So perhaps in a previous life—which I haven't dealt in with Bonn Jovi, I haven't gone back that far with him—perhaps he had been a human, perhaps he was a sage at one point, a person. Being able to communicate with animals, and able to go into their past lives, I know that some *have* been humans. They have told me about their past lives. Some animals have been human at certain times, and they have decided because of the freedom or the beauty and gracefulness of a horse, and their life as a human was so harsh, that they chose to come back in the body of a horse. And these animals are not necessarily only horses. Animals have had many past lives. They have reincarnated and reincarnated in different species. If you are a rat, for instance, and have gone into the spirit world you could come back as a butterfly. Longevity is not usually what you want, you just want to keep reincarnating, you want to keep coming back as different species, for the experience. So I don't have a problem with wondering how Bonn Jovi does poetry.

———————

During my research I came across many anecdotes concerning the reincarnation of animals to the same owner. This one is from Sue Goodrich, a communicator who lives in Escondido, a suburb of San Diego:

A man contacted me who was very depressed. He said all he had had in his life was his dog, who had died a year before. He had lost his religious beliefs, and his marriage was falling apart. I was able to contact the dog in spirit, and it said it wanted to come back. I told the man, but this idea was foreign to him.

I told him the dog had said she wanted to come back as she was before, a cocker mix. I told him to look in the newspaper for puppies of that sort. I told him that the dog's spirit said she would present herself to him. A friend of the man took this seriously and went looking for litters like this. He would lay the guy's shirt down to see if any of the puppies would come over. And sure enough, in one litter a male puppy came and sat right on the shirt. He took the puppy back to the man's house. As soon as he brought him in, the dog ran to the bedroom, went under the bed, and got his dish. And all the other animals in the house were going like, "Oh hi, you're back."

The man called a priest he had known when he was close to his religion, and the priest said, "Absolutely, your dog is back." [A hip priest, psychologically or parapsychologically, or both.]

The man got back into his religion and renewed his friendship with this priest. He made up with his wife, and he says he has never been so happy. He says he thanks the dog every day for giving him that lesson.

———————

Mary Esther Borie, an animal communicator based in Santa Rosa, California, gave me an account of an animal she feels came back to her personally:

I have a cat that's been with me before in this lifetime. I had him originally when I was a teenager. He was an orange and white tabby with long hair. He was a very big and beautiful cat. I called him Jean-Tom. When I was in my late thirties I kept getting visions of an orange and white cat. I wasn't remembering Jean-Tom, because that was such a long time ago.

Then my neighbors across the street, a father and grown son, got a kitten that was orange and white. They called him Zachary. He wouldn't stay there; he kept coming over to my house. He would sit in the kitchen and say, "Can I have some of that food?" He'd get up on the bed and go to sleep, make himself at home. I'd have to take him home, walk him across the street, and say, "Your kitten was visiting with me."

When I'd bring him back he'd get really angry with me. One day the kitty came to me and he had an abscess in his chest and an abscess in his foot, from getting in a cat fight. I took him in and started taking care of his wounds, and he was so happy to let me. So I went across the street and said, "You know, your cat wants to live with me."

And they said, "Oh we don't care, you can have him."

And one day after that he said, "Don't you remember me?" Then it came to me. I said, "I know who you are, you were Jean-Tom."

When I asked Anita Curtis, a communicator who lives in Gilbertsville, Pennsylvania, for accounts involving animals who had died, she gave me two anecdotes. Here they are:

A dog had been hit by a car and killed. His owner had heard of Anita's abilities and called her.

"The man had been devastated about losing the dog," Anita told me. "Someone had suggested that he call me to try to get in contact with the dog. I contacted the dog in spirit, and he said he would be back in six months as a golden retriever. He had been a mix. The dog said that when he came back he would give the man a sign. The man didn't really believe me; he indicated politely that he thought I was full of it.

"However, he called me back several months later to tell me that he had gotten a golden retriever puppy. He said it had some of the characteristics of the other dog, but he wasn't sure. But something had just happened that he wanted to ask me about. He said his wife worked in a nursing home, and that she used to take the original dog to work with her. The staff at the nursing home had given the dog his own name tag, but he had lost it.

"When the new puppy was old enough, the man's wife had taken it to work with her. The first day, the puppy immediately went to a pile of stuff, dove into it, and came up with the old dog's name tag, which had been missing for months. The man wanted to know if I considered that a sign. I told him that I thought it was—the new dog knew where the name tag was.

"The man asked me when I gave workshops and said he wanted to learn how to communicate. This was quite a turnaround for him."

———

Some people are very emotionally dependent on their animals, even after the animal has died. A woman had asked Anita to contact her dead dog. The dog, Anita told me, had said he would come back, but not before six months.

"About three weeks ago," Anita said, "the woman called me up early in the morning, and she was frantic. She had lost her car keys and she asked if the dog could tell her where they were."

I asked Anita if the dog had done that when he was alive.

"I don't think so," she replied, "but this woman depends a lot on this dog now."

Fascinated, I told Anita to continue. She told me:

The first word I got from the dog's spirit was "kitchen." The woman said she thought so too, and she had searched the kitchen and they weren't there. The next thing I got from the dog was a picture of an upholstered chair. I asked her if she had such a chair in the kitchen. She said no, but she used to. She had upholstered chairs in the living room, and she searched them, but there was nothing there.

So she went back to the kitchen and looked where the upholstered chair used to be, and she got down and looked under a bookcase next to where the chair had been, and there she found her keys.

"Does she still have the chair?" I asked Anita.

"No, her ex-husband took it with him when he left."

"That's a good way to find keys," I said.

"Of course," Anita replied, "just ask a dead dog."

The key-finding dog had been a black Labrador retriever. He had told Anita he was coming back to the woman again as a black Lab.

"I suppose she will go around looking for black Lab puppies," I said.

"Yes," Anita said, "and one will choose her. That's not unusual. There might be a litter of puppies and one will come over and plop itself on your lap, or reach out and touch you, or something like that. That'll be the dog. That happens a lot."

An interesting example of a reincarnating animal making its presence known to its former owners is embodied in this account from Becky Ferris, an animal communicator who lives in that bastion of left-brained thinking, Los Alamos, New Mexico, birthplace of the atom bomb. The Ferrises had several animals, including three wolves. They also owned a Netherland Dwarf Blue rabbit.

"We called her Mouse," Becky says. "She was little and gray, she didn't even weigh a pound. One day she was killed by one of our wolves."

Some weeks after Mouse's demise, Becky's husband asked her to communicate with Mouse's spirit. He missed Mouse and wanted to know if she wanted to come back and live with them. Mouse said she did. Becky told me:

> She goes, "Just look in the paper." We looked in the paper and there was an ad for Netherland Dwarf Blues. We went to the place, and this lady had about fifty rabbits in a pen. There was a two-foot-high fence around the pen. I had asked Mouse, "How will we know it's you?" And she said, "Oh, you'll know."
>
> When we got there, all of a sudden this little bitty bunny came running from the other side of this pen and crawled up this two-foot fence to get to us.
>
> The lady wondered why this little rabbit would do this. I didn't tell her, because Los Alamos is a very scientific community. Psychic stuff is very frowned on around here.
>
> The lady said, "I just know this rabbit belongs to you, and I'm not going to charge you."

When we brought her home, all the animals knew it was Mouse. They gave her kisses and were so happy to have her back.

———————

I asked Denise Kinch, a professional communicator who lives in Groveland, Massachusetts, if she had had experiences involving reincarnation of animals, and she told me, "Most of the animals I've dealt with have come back, but I didn't know them previously. Most have told me that they want to come back to their owners, when their owners are ready. The only one I knew previously was a pony that belonged to some neighbors down the road, the Eskels. It was a pony then, and it has come back as their dog."

I spoke with both Denise and another woman, Carol Eskel, about this happening. Denise told me:

I did a lot of communication with the horse, who was called Champagne, before she died, and she said she wanted to come back, but in a different form. About a year after her death, we went out to buy

Carrie and Sara Eskel with Rikki, whom they say used to be their pony

a Belgian shepherd, and there was no question it was the horse. I knew it by telepathy, and Carol and her two kids knew it because a lot of the mannerisms of the dog resembled things the pony had done— the way she followed people in the family, the way she greeted them, the body postures. Mostly body positions—the dog is more like a pony than she is like a dog. Carol and the kids all said, "That's Champagne." There were nine puppies, but there was no question that we were supposed to take this puppy.

Carol Eskel corroborated what Denise had told me, and added some interesting touches. Denise had invited Sue Goodrich of Escondido, California, to come to Massachusetts and give a training workshop on animal communication. Champagne had been in poor health, and Carol asked Sue to talk with the pony.

Carol told me, "Sue said the pony told her she was going to be leaving, but that she'd be back in a year. I wondered how she was going to do that, because I wasn't planning on getting another horse. But our family dog had died about a year later, and I decided to get another dog. I wanted to get a Belgian shepherd, and we heard of a breeder in Maine. I asked Denise to come along, because she is more knowledgeable about dogs than us." They chose the dog, whom they call Rikki, from nine eight-week-old puppies. "But it was more once we got home," Carol says, "that we noticed things.

"When I took her out of the car," Carol says, "there was a kid riding one of our horses in our riding ring. The puppy was on a leash, but she began dragging at it, she wanted to get over to the ring to see the horse. She had known that horse when she was Champagne; it was one of her buddies.

"She settled in like she had always lived here. We didn't go through the usual puppy adjustment—carrying on at night. Usually the first few nights a puppy will cry all night; they're lonely or whatever. She didn't do any of that.

"We took her down to the barn with us, and during the first week or so she would roll in the shavings. Champagne always did that. Dogs don't normally roll in shavings."

I told Carol about Denise's description of Rikki's body postures, which seemed to her more those of a pony than a dog. Carol laughed and said, "That's correct. We do some agility work with the dog. She loves jumping, and the pony did too. This dog will jump higher than she is tall."

———————

During one of our talks, Denise Kinch mentioned that there are sometimes variations to be considered in the return of animals from former lives. "I find," she said, "that sometimes there can be a partial part of a spirit of the past animal come back, not the whole spirit. There can be a combination with another spirit. There are also things that happen that are called walk-ins.

"I had a Doberman dog that had died," Denise went on. "I got a new Doberman puppy. Sue Goodrich told me that if I really wanted my first Doberman to come back into the body of the new puppy, she could. All three of us—the two dogs and myself—would have to agree on it, Sue said. I didn't agree to it. I respect each individual as it is. Although I loved my other Doberman very much, I would not want to send this new dog's spirit away to get the first one's back. I understand this happens in people a lot, also. It happens in animals if an owner is really grieving and really wants that animal back, and can't get over it. Then it does occasionally happen. The spirit of the animal the person has at that time will agree to leave, and the old one will come back."

The subject of walk-ins struck a chord with me, because I know two people who seem to be involved in such a situation. One is a woman named Ann Valukis, who lives in Natick, Massachusetts. The other is Alex Tanous, a world-famous psychic who died a few years ago. He lived in Portland, Maine, and often taught on parapsychology at the University of Maine. I interviewed Alex twice over the years and put him in two of my books on ghosts and parapsychology.

Ann is a medium and a great admirer of Alex. Recently I had heard that Ann was receiving messages—love letters, in fact—from Alex through a word processor. I checked this out with Ann, and found that it certainly seemed to be true. He was coming through the word processor of a friend of Ann's, whom I also know, a former high school principal.

The word processor aspect was rather startling, but more pertinent to this discussion is that the spirit of Alex was also purportedly doing walk-ins. Ann told me that he had spent a few months in the body of a young man who had since died of AIDS. But at present, Alex was residing in the body of a professional man who practiced in a western suburb of Boston. I had read of walk-ins, but this was the first time I had known the people supposedly involved.

I am not particularly psychic myself. But I have been interested in the field for almost thirty years, and have developed a wide, superficial observer's knowledge that sometimes makes me a better detective than people who can actually do it. And with this preamble, let me present the story of two greyhounds—or is it one?—in Cincinnati.

They were owned by Barbara Wright, a writer and publisher who detests the use of animals in sporting events. Racing greyhounds are particularly abused, she feels. She has three greyhounds she has acquired through rescue organizations.

At one time she had a dog she called Echo. When Echo died of leukemia, Barbara took it very hard, but she had an intuition Echo would be back, that Echo was waiting for her. She immediately went in search of a dog like Echo, a red fawn female greyhound.

She went to a rescue league that had a group of greyhounds that had been brought in from a racetrack in West Virginia. She chose a red fawn with black coloring, a brindle. Before long, she began to suspect the second dog was the first dog—reincarnated. She even named it Echo.

She engaged a well-known Cincinnati animal communicator, Donetta Zimmerman, to come to her home and check out her three dogs, in a routine health and happiness sort of way. She told Donetta nothing of her suspicions about Echo. I received my first information on this case from Donetta, who told me, "Barbara had three greyhounds. I got good information out of the first two. The third, Echo, described a life she had had being raised by two ladies in New Hampshire who were very nice to her. They were racing trainers. The dog said she had had a problem with her back and was retired from racing."

When Donetta described this life to Barbara, Barbara said, "That's not the life *this* dog had. That was the life my first dog had, a pleasant life in which two women were good to her. *This* dog had a horrible life." It had lived under terrible conditions; it had almost starved. Its owner had gone bankrupt, and finally his dogs had been confiscated by the Humane Society, or a similar agency. The dog had found its way to Barbara through a rescue-adoption agency.

Barbara told me that Donetta had had no prior awareness of the history of any of the dogs she had met at Barbara's house.

I asked Barbara why she was so sure that Echo I had returned. She provided some impressive particulars, for example:

She plays in the same way as Echo I.
She plays in the same part of the dining room.
She has the same expression.
She puts me to bed the same way my first Echo put me to bed.
Her mannerisms, gestures, facial expressions are the same as the
     first Echo.

Barbara also said, "The second Echo told Donetta about running on the beach with me. When I lived in Salem, Massachusetts, I ran on the beach with the first Echo every night. The second Echo told about driving all night on the backseat of my car when we came from Salem to Cincinnati. She told Donetta a lot of things about the two women she had lived with in New Hampshire."

After mulling over this information from Donetta and Barbara, I began to wonder if this could be a walk-in. It seemed to have many of the characteristics: an owner who had been devastated by her first dog's death; a second dog who had had a difficult life and probably would be willing, even glad, to get out of its body; and the spirit of a dog who wanted to come back to its owner.

When Donetta worked with Echo II, she saw no indication whatever of the second Echo's actual, unhappy life. It seemed as though that life was not in the mind of the dog at all. What Donetta gathered through telepathy was the pleasant life of Echo I. It would seem that both dogs, and Barbara Wright, were happy to agree to the walk-in, the switch of souls.

When I broached the subject of my walk-in theory to Donetta and Barbara, they both readily agreed. So readily, in fact, that I suspected that they had felt this all along, but probably didn't want to suggest to me an idea so outlandish.

II

Ghosts of Animals

Do animals have ghosts?

    Having written six books involving ghosts of humans, I must say it seems logical to me that they do.

I am accustomed to people asking me, "Have *you* ever seen a ghost—of a human being *or* an animal?" My rather defensive reply comes in two parts, beginning with, "No, but . . ."

The first phase of my two-part answer is that I have investigated some two hundred cases of supposed hauntings, and interviewed close to a thousand people who say they have seen ghosts, heard ghosts, smelled them, sensed them, touched or been touched by them, or all of the above. These people do not impress me as being crazy, or even mildly flaky. Most of them seem solid citizens, with nothing to gain by claiming to be aware of visitors from an adjacent dimension. In fact, some might have something to lose.

Other people, whom I was not interviewing, friends and casual acquaintances, knowing my predilection for the next world, tell me of experiences they have had of ghosts. I have a friend who says she doesn't believe in ghosts. Her problem is that she keeps seeing them. I've never gotten it clear on how she reconciles this situation.

The second part of my defense for not personally seeing ghosts, yet writing about them, is that when I'm working on books about hauntings, poltergeist phenomena happen all around me, usually in my workroom. This does not happen when I'm writing books about other subjects. But when I'm doing a book on ghosts, research disappears— then reappears if I'm lucky. A roll of film dissipates into thin air, never to be seen again. It was there on the desk one moment, not there the next, even though unfortunately I wasn't watching at the moment of its disappearance. A chapter goes missing from a finished manuscript, then reappears when a talented medium places the blame, and I reprimand the spirit who is responsible. I do not have to take this last fascinating incident at secondhand—it happened to me.

Strange things happen on my phone, especially when I'm taping an interview. Occasionally the tape will be backward, sometimes parts of it will be faint. On one tape, I was interviewing a woman by phone about her lover—a famous dancer—who had died not long before. When I played the tape back later I noticed that the woman's voice was clear and strong when we spoke about general subjects related to dance, such as a tour of South American dancers she was planning, or a famed dance troupe I had seen in Mexico City. But when I asked specific questions about her deceased lover, there was silence on the tape during the time she was replying, even though I'd heard her clearly during the actual interview. Later on in the tape, when I would ask another general question, her voice would again be there. It seemed obvious that her lover did not want to be in that book. He was in it, and so was a recapitulation of this incident, but I didn't use his name.

Early in my career of investigating the occult, I visited Elwood Babbitt, a psychic who lives in western Massachusetts. He had considerable livestock on his property, and he mentioned casually that often some of his deceased ponies could be seen galloping through his living room. When I got home, I told this to my wife, and she said, "They must have made an awful mess." She was a sly joker type.

One of my first books on the occult, *The Ghostly Register*, included the ghosts of a cat and a rat. I titled the cat chapter, "Some Cats Aren't Satisfied with Nine Lives." The cat, along with several human ghosts, inhabited an elegant Victorian mansion in Midland Park, New Jersey. Several people have reported seeing it, a yellow and white kitty. Many others say they have felt it, or at least some sort of furry critter. And hundreds of other people have reported feeling warm spots where the cat had lain—and possibly still was present. Feeling the warm spots seems to be a popular entertainment in Midland Park.

The owner of the house from 1952 to 1979 was Ethelyn Woodlock, an eminent painter. The ghostly cat hung out in a small third-story room. Mrs. Woodlock said that during her time she had had four different beds in the room, but the cat adjusted nicely, leaving its warm spot on each bed in turn. The house has been investigated by famous parapsychologists, including Karlis Osis, Keith Harary, and Ingo Swann.

It might be noteworthy that Mrs. Woodlock considered herself a psychic painter, and often did illustrations involving ghosts. It seems something of an axiom that when psychic people live in a place, the place is then observed to be haunted. They are aware of things many of us are not. Perhaps in some cases such people even draw in spirits.

This theory seems operative in the case of the rat ghost, observed in the village of Genesee, Idaho, by a lady who admits to psychic proclivities. She is Sara Joyce, who told me, "I have an Indian heritage. My father's mother was Indian. The psychic orientation is quite strong."

Soon after Sara bought a building on the main street of town, she and her family found that it was inhabited by various human spirits. But the high point of this chapter for me has always been the rat. To quote Sara:

One morning early, I came down the stairs, turned the corner into the kitchen doorway, and quick as lightning something jumped up onto my arm. It was a rat! A huge, silvery, shiny, golden, transparent rat. It had an abundance of hair, and I felt its claws on my skin as it climbed up my arm. When I screamed, it disappeared. I stood on the spot several minutes in disbelief. How could this have been? I began to doubt whether I had really seen it, looking at my arm to see if there were marks on my skin. There were no visual marks, but I could still feel the sensation of claws pricking my skin.

After I had moved out of the building to a house in Genesee, a very calm and quiet house, so far completely free of noises and presences, my son Bill returned from Hawaii and moved into the old apartment to do some remodeling and restructuring of the space. When he lifted up some of the floorboards in the kitchen under the sink, there lay a huge rat mummy, complete with a quantity of hair and a long, bushy tail. We theorized that this rat had long ago died under the floorboards there and that somehow its spirit had released itself at the very moment I entered the kitchen, using my arm on its upward path, up and away!

When one is researching the occult, one finds that animals figure in ghost stories in a couple of possible ways. Sometimes they are ghosts themselves, other times they are live witnesses. I often consider dogs as the most trustworthy of witnesses. Dogs never lie. If a dog is scared by a place, I'm very prone to believe that it's haunted.

A haunted theater I wrote about in Tupelo, Mississippi, had both aspects of animal participation—both as a ghost and as a witness. The manager of the theater, Mike Curtis, told me of an experience his wife, Vicki, had had while cleaning the premises. She had opened a closet in the projection booth and could hear strange sounds.

Vicki told me, "There were dogs barking. My sister was with me that night. You'd close the broom closet and you wouldn't hear anything. Open it and it would sound like seven or eight dogs barking. It was just your normal closet; all it had in it was brooms and a utility sink. It just happened that one time."

On another night, Vicki took her Doberman, Raven, along to the theater as a bodyguard. Raven was as psychic as the next dog, and something scared him in a very serious way. It might have been one of the suspected human ghosts in the place, but it might have been the unseen noisy barkers. At any rate, Vicki declared:

Everything was OK downstairs, and I started to go upstairs to check the projection booth. When I started up the stairs, every hair on that Doberman's back stood up. I didn't see or hear anything, but she started growling and showing her teeth, and that's something this dog never does. But she just went crazy that night. I had her on a chain and had the chain wrapped around my hand. That dog tore the chain off my hand and just cut my hand all up. She took off and she hit the heavy glass front door so hard that she shoved that thing open—and those things aren't easy to open. She ran outside, clear down to the road. I finally caught up to her and got her into the car. I went back into the theater because I had to turn the lights out and lock the door. She would not get out of the car, so I didn't even try getting her out. She stayed in the car, and she barked, and she howled, and she growled the whole time I was in the theater. I could hear her while I was inside; I had left the door open—I wasn't going in there with the door closed. And I had to take her home. The next night I took her and she never did a thing. It wasn't that she was frightened of the theater, because she was in the theater almost every night with me.

I asked Vicki if she had checked to see if anyone was in the theater, and she said she hadn't, but added, "Raven wasn't afraid of people, she wouldn't have barked and growled at a person."

It might be worth noting that Vicki is apparently psychic. She and her daughter, Ann, say they can communicate at a distance. One of them just thinks of the other, and then they get on the phone.

―――――――――――

Pierre van Paassen was a popular Dutch writer some decades ago. Van Paassen wrote about a personal experience he says he had with the ghost of a dog—a very active one. He said that he was sitting in his house one evening in an upstairs room with two neighbors. Suddenly they heard the patter of an animal's feet. They went to the top of the stairs, and at the bottom was a big, black dog. They started down the stairs, and the dog faded away—disappeared.

After that, van Paassen wrote, it often came back, always about eleven o'clock at night. The author said he once felt the dog before he saw it. He was going up the stairs and felt it brush against him. Then he saw it. The dog was going down the stairs he had just come up.

One evening, van Paassen brought two of his own dogs into the house, and stood with them at the foot of the steps. Soon the sound of paws was heard crossing the floor above. Van Paassen did not see the ghostly dog that night, but he was sure it was there. He saw his two dogs in vigorous battle with something invisible, and the live dogs seemed to be getting the worst of it.

A dog witness story similar to the one in the Tupelo movie house came to my attention involving a little theater about ten miles from where I live in a suburb of Boston. I put it in my book *A Ghosthunter's Guide.*

The Vokes Theatre, located in Wayland, Massachusetts, has long been inhabited by a group of amateur theater buffs. It was built in 1904 by a professional English actress who had married a well-heeled American and moved to Wayland. She had built this little theater, a charming show in itself, and later donated it to the locals. Her name was Beatrice Herford. She named the theater after a well-known English comedienne of the time, Rosina Vokes.

Beatrice knew many theatrical luminaries of her time, and autographed pictures of people like Katherine Cornell, Ellen Terry, Lotte Crabtree, George Arliss, Nora Bayes, and Ethel Barrymore adorn the walls. Even more prominent is a large portrait of Beatrice, who died in 1952. It hangs at the end of the lobby.

Many believe that Beatrice is haunting the Vokes. I'm pretty sure I do. And so, it would appear, did a certain German shepherd. His person, Bobbsie Mitton, has long been active in the theater group. She told me:

You know the portrait of Beatrice Herford that's hung in the lobby? I had a very big German shepherd named Jeffie who was just a kind of easygoing critter, and he was over there with me one evening when I was going to a rehearsal. I walked in the door and he came in behind me, turned right, and he came to a screeching halt. He stared at the picture, backed up, turned around, went flipping out the door, and I couldn't get him to go back in the theater.

This was a serious kind of dog. He'd sit around the yard kind of mellow, complacent. He looked like he wanted to become a lawyer. But this night I had to put him in the car. He was transfixed.

Having mined my past research for animal ghosts and witnesses, let me now turn my attention to ghost stories I've encountered while interviewing animal communicators for this present book.

Jim Worsley, an animal communicator who lives in Richmond, Virginia, gave me the story of the ghost of a kitty who was being mean to a cat it had lived with for several years. Jim told me:

> I had this client last year in Ohio who had a problem with her cat not going to the litter box. It turned out that a cat who had lived there a long time and who had just died used to tease the other cat around the litter box. This was when they were both alive. The two cats lived together five or six years.
>
> It turned out that the essence—or spirit—of the dead cat was still around, and the live cat was afraid to go to the litter box because it would get teased by the spirit. The ghost was still playing games. So we just suggested that they make peace with each other. We told the dead cat that it could go on to where it needed to go now. As far as I know, the person hasn't had a problem with the live cat avoiding the litter box since then.

Mischief from the next world is not confined to animal spirits, human spirits also do quite well at it, according to Mary Esther Borie, a communicator from Santa Rosa, California.

"Animals are sensitive to seeing ghosts," she told me. "I can see them too, but a lot of people can't. One lady called me from Washington State. She was having a very difficult time emotionally because her dog was barking so much that the neighbors were complaining. She'd had notices about keeping her dog quiet. She loved her little dog and she was feeling pressure that she would have to get rid of him. The dog was barking both inside and outside the house. Even inside, the barking was so loud it bothered the neighbors. She called me to ask, why is my dog barking so much?

"So I talked with the little dog, and he was very upset because there was the spirit of the woman's deceased husband in the house. The woman was not aware that his spirit was around. The man was very possessive of her. She had remarried and then divorced and had had other animals. Whenever she had a person or an animal around, her husband's spirit would try to get rid of them. She had already gone through two or three dogs. One was killed in front of the house. All these tragic things were happening."

I asked Mary Esther if she felt the ghost was making these things happen.

"Apparently this was what was going on," she replied. "There was an influence exerted by this spirit. The spirit didn't like the dog being around because the dog was getting his wife's love and attention."

I asked Mary Esther what she had done about the situation.

"It was time to move the spirit on," she replied. "I told the woman, 'You're going to have to ask him to leave.' I instruct people how to do that. And I told the dog, too. I said, 'Anytime you even feel his energy, you ask him to leave.'

"It was imperative that the woman take the responsibility, and that she move the spirit forward. I told her, 'You ask him to take the next step, to move and grow.' And this worked."

I asked Mary Esther if she worked with other beings, such as angels, guides, or whatever.

"I can," she said, "if the situation warrants it. If I feel the angels need to intervene, then I will ask them to. But importantly, most of the time, I want people to learn that they have the ability to do this themselves."

Mary Esther Borie and Katy

Donetta Zimmerman, the Cincinnati communicator, told me about two women who had an experience with a deceased dog who wanted to help a friend make the transition to the next world. The women's names were Anna Roo and Pat North. Donetta told me:

They had three dogs. These were Kelly, a very old chow, who was ready to go; a young male chow that was very strong; and a very old schnauzer who was blind. When it was time for Kelly to go, the women wanted to be sure they were doing the right thing before they had her put to sleep. So they had me come and talk to Kelly one last time. She said, "Yes, I'm ready to go. My friend is going to come after me."

The night before they took her to the vet, the women were in the house with the three dogs and for no apparent reason the old chow started smiling. The blind schnauzer jumped up and started wagging his tail like he was seeing an old friend. And the very young chow started barking at a blank wall.

The women said they felt the presence of their original chow dog, and they believed he was coming to get Kelly. The next day they took Kelly to the vet, and they felt very comfortable about it.

I talked with Anna Roo for her view of the occurrence, and she said, "From what the dogs told Donetta, the big red dog did come to get Kelly. He was another chow we had owned, and he died of cancer. He's come back a couple of times. The dogs we have now see him. He wants to play with the live dogs but is unable to, but they know he's here.

"We have a lot of things that go on with dogs that come back here. Once while I was going to bed, I glanced out into the hall and there were four red paws. The body started forming from the paws up. One of our dogs, Bear, who was deceased, slowly started being re-created. I freaked out and went into bed. I could see him very well. I jumped into bed before his head became visible, but I knew it was Bear, because he had very distinct markings. I was frightened by this."

Both women are intuitive, and are aware of ghostly dogs in the house, but Anna is particularly psychic. She comes from a family in which psychic activity has always been routine. I asked her why they bring in

Donetta when they can be aware of, and even talk with, the deceased animals themselves.

"I guess," Anna said, "it's because the dogs are real close to us, and sometimes it's unnerving when you're that close to them emotionally. And we're not as well trained as Donetta. We get much more depth with Donetta. We can just do it on a surface level. From Donetta, we can get background history on the dogs, what's happened to them, how they feel today."

———————

Kate Solisti, a communicator who lives in Santa Fe but who travels widely, told me a delightful account of an adventure with a spectral schnauzer. It happened in England, that country where spotting specters is something of a national pastime. Kate put the story this way:

When I go to England, I stay with a lady named Lavender Dower, who is eighty-eight years old. She lives in a four hundred-year-old cottage in the Cotswalds. She used to have a sister named Rosemary, and the villagers called them the Herbs.

Lavender had a partner, and they treated animals radionically for years. That's a type of energetic healing. Lavender has a thriving—and I mean *thriving*—practice. She treats the finest horses in Great Britain. Lavender's partner died and left her two schnauzers. They got elderly and one of them died. Lavender saw the first schnauzer meet her deceased partner in the garden and they disappeared, they went off together.

Lavender had the feeling that the second little dog was sticking around to take care of her. The dog didn't trust the two Siamese cats to do a good job of it. The house, incidentally, has the ghost of an old monk, but I've never seen him. When I came to the house, I said, "I'm not interested in seeing any ghosts of people. I just can't deal with that. But I'm fine with animals."

One evening when I was clearing the table I was taking dishes from the dining room to the kitchen and I went through a foyer between the two rooms. A young woman was having dinner with us and she had arrived with her dog, a big German shepherd puppy called Bea. As I was crossing the foyer, I heard footsteps behind me and I assumed it was Bea. In front of me there was a Dutch door, with glass in the upper part of it. I looked in the glass to see if it was Bea, and I saw the reflection of a very small black schnauzer. When I turned around, all I saw was a little shadow, and then it was gone. That was the only time that I myself have seen a ghost. She was just checking up on me. Apparently she follows everybody around in the house.

———————

One day while I was researching this chapter, I received a short note from Barbara Meyers, an animal communicator who lives on Staten Island, across New York Bay from Manhattan. The note said, "A person who has had 'solid' visitations from animals who have crossed over is Dr. Alan Sacerdote, of Brooklyn." And she provided a phone number. The note was cryptic but intriguing. I called the number, and a man answered. I asked if this was Dr. Sacerdote, and he said it was.

"Are you a veterinarian?" I asked.

"No," he replied, chuckling, "I'm a human endocrinologist."

Feeling a bit at a loss, I stumbled on. "Barbara Meyers sent me a note about you," I said. "Well, tell me what you know."

Barbara Meyers

"I'll tell you what we experienced," he replied. "That's the best I can do."

This struck me as one of the more perceptive comments I'd heard lately. We all experience so much and *know* so little.

"When our first cat, Tabatha, passed away," he went on, "about the second day after her death we noticed that food that we hadn't cleaned up from her plate, most of it was gone. It was as though Tabatha was making contact with us. We'd had her for over seventeen years."

"How many people were in the house?" I asked.

"Four."

"You and your wife? . . ."

"And our two children."

"How old are the children?"

"Currently they're twenty-one and seventeen. This goes back about five years."

"How do you know someone wasn't playing a joke?"

"We didn't have any visitors during that time. And I really think all of us in the family were too grief-stricken to have played a joke like that."

"Was it cat food?"

"Yes. We were all kind of depressed, and nobody had the heart to clean up her dish. That was just the beginning."

"What happened then?"

"We buried her out in the yard, and one night about a week afterward I was looking out the window at where Tabatha was buried and—this could be a total hallucination—but what I saw just above where she'd been buried was a bluish purple whirlwind. That's the only way I could describe it. Other people, including Barbara [Meyers], have remarked that as they passed by that they noticed a kind of shimmering energy over the spot where she was buried.

"I've also seen her," Alan went on. "On rare occasions, full face. More often, out of the corner of my eye. My son has never had visions of her; he may be a little more hardheaded than the rest of us. My wife would see her for about six months or a year after her death, out of the corner of her eye. My daughter and I still do."

"At your home?" I asked.

"Yes," he replied. "On occasion, there were other things she would do. You would hear a meow, without there being any cat in the house—any physical cat. Her smell would appear very strongly. In a closed room, we have a couple of ficus trees—tropical houseplants. Normally, there's no wind in the house in the wintertime, all the doors and windows are closed. So the leaves of the trees will just drop around the pot that the trees are in. But there was a leaf that seemed to have been moved almost deliberately right into the center of the floor of the living room.

"When Tabatha was alive, she used to do quite a bit of spitting up of hair balls. A few days after she died there was a new cat spit-up stain on the carpet. This is the kind of thing that has been happening since she passed away in 1990.

"Subsequently, we had another cat, whom we named Zoe. She died in kittenhood of an infectious peritonitis. We got very attached to her too. Her visitations were kind of different.

"The first thing she did was the same day she died. After she had died, my daughter saw her going down the steps to the landing where the litter box was. It was an astral Zoe going down to use the litter box."

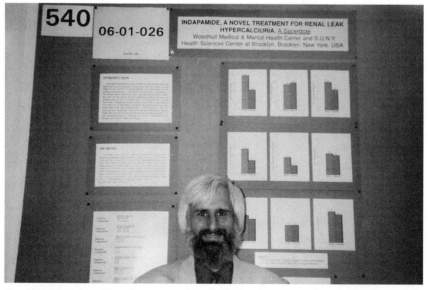

Dr. Alan Sacerdote. The photo was taken during a presentation by Dr. Sacerdote at an international congress of endocrinology, in Nice, France. Dr. Sacerdote notes: "I thought that the seeming contradiction of a clinical researcher who sometimes sees ghosts might add a little spice."

He said Barbara Meyers, who is a friend of the family and often visits the house, had also seen Zoe. I spoke to Barbara and she mentioned such an incident.

"I saw Zoe walking across the kitchen," she said. "She was solid, but not defined. She walked into the pantry and out of sight. I was sitting with Alan in the kitchen, and he saw her too."

Alan mentioned an occurrence when he was observing the anniversary of Zoe's death with a Judaic ceremony called Yahrzeit. "I lit a candle on a counter," he said. "About five minutes after I had lit this memorial candle, another object on the counter—I don't remember what it was—just moved toward the candle."

I asked Alan if he and his family have had other psychic experiences, and he said yes. He described several experiences on the part of his wife, his daughter, and himself.

It occurred to me that in the course of research on previous books about ghosts, I had found that when there is more than one intuitive person in a house—they are usually related to each other—that psychic manifestations seem not only to occur, but to proliferate. A highly regarded medium once told me that the energies of more than one psychic person can combine to make it easier for a being from another plane to break through the veil separating the dimensions, and to manifest in some way in our physical dimension. This may be what was happening in the Sacerdote household.

12

Finding Lost Animals Through Telepathy

Communicators often told me that finding missing animals can be a frustrating and thankless task, and that many take pains to avoid such jobs.

"Finding lost animals is one of the most difficult things you can do," Phil Roberts of Maine said. "About 80 percent of the time, the animal is dead, and it's a really unhappy time, it becomes more involved with counseling of the people. Sometimes the animal is alive, but just doesn't want to come home, and people don't want to hear that; they won't listen when you tell them that. Finding lost animals is really a toughie."

I asked Phil if he had had any successes at all with lost animals.

"Sometimes I do," he said. "It's more likely to be successful if they call me really quick. One time a friend called me. They were hiking. The dog would go off by himself, but he always came back after a few minutes. This time he didn't come back. They called me within a half hour. They had parked their van before they started out on their hike. I contacted the dog telepathically and told him to go to the van. By the time they got back to the van, the dog was there."

I do like it here, but I'm ready for my own apartment.
Drawing by Leo Cullum; © 1996 The New Yorker Magazine, Inc.

Sometimes a missing animal isn't lost—it just doesn't want to be found. For one reason or another, it feels it is time to move on. Judy Meyer of Santa Fe, New Mexico, put it like this:

Cats and dogs tell me that not every relationship is meant to last a lifetime. Just like with people. Sometimes when cats and dogs have gone, they have just chosen to go and live with other people. Not that you did anything wrong. It's like that they came to do a job with you, and then they go to the next job. I've had cats of my own leave and go to live with other people. People can't imagine animals wanting to leave their homes, but the animals know what they're doing.

I mentioned to Judy that I had heard constantly along the way that some animals are spirits who are there to help us.

"Of course they are," she replied. "This is the essence of what your book should be explaining to people—that these are very intelligent beings who have come here to do work with us, who bring us many gifts, who are teachers. Some of it is that we need to take care of them, some of it is that they take care of us, some of it is that they are showing us how we are feeling about people." Judy went on to tell me this story:

A woman in Santa Fe named Sylvia called me and said she was missing Kiwi, her twelve-year-old cat. I talked to the cat telepathically, and she described the area around her house perfectly. She said she had gone up a ridge behind her house and down a ridge, and now she's going to town. I told this to the woman, and she was very relieved that the cat hadn't gone into the woods and been eaten by a coyote.

"No," I said, "She's walking to town."

Kiwi wouldn't agree to come home, so I asked her why. She said that nobody had asked her about the move to Santa Fe. Nobody had asked her how she liked the new house. And on top of that, there were houseguests in her new space. Sylvia confirmed to me that there were indeed houseguests. She apologized to Kiwi, but the cat still wouldn't agree to come home. So I advised Sylvia to do all the practical things—put an ad in the newspaper, put out signs with her phone number and a description of Kiwi, call the Humane Society, and see what happened. Nothing happened. Sylvia had put out signs, but she put them in front of her own house. I told her that wouldn't work, she'd have to put the signs in various parts of town. She did, but still no Kiwi. The third time I talked with this cat, I finally got smart. I asked her, "What is the real purpose for your leaving?"

And Kiwi, speaking to Sylvia through me, said, "I am showing you what it feels like to be missing that piece of your heart that is keeping you from experiencing the total story of living. It has to do with your father."

Up to now, Sylvia had been very calm with me, but now she just broke down and started crying on the phone. She said, "There's no way you would have known this. My father died when I was fourteen. I've always known I've been missing this piece of my heart. My heart is broken. I've always meant to do something about it, but I never did."

So I said to Kiwi, "Would you come home if Sylvia went and did some heart healing work?" And Kiwi said yes.

The next day, Sylvia went to a man who did therapy through the use of crystals, and she said she was greatly helped by this treatment. That evening, she talked with Kiwi through Judy. According to Judy, Kiwi then furnished the names of the streets in the area in which she was hanging out.

"You mean," I asked Judy, "that Kiwi can read street signs?"

Judy didn't seem completely sure about this, but she did mention the names of a couple of the streets that Kiwi had identified. From these clues, Judy deduced that Kiwi was in the neighborhood of a local institution called St. John's College. She urged Sylvia to go over there and put up some Kiwi signs.

By the next morning, Judy told me, Kiwi was back, brought by a man who was connected with the college and who had seen the signs. He told Sylvia, "The cat came right up to me and allowed me to pick her up."

Carol Gurney of Agoura, California, is a well-known animal communicator who estimates that she has taught the art to over one thousand people in the past nine years. She teaches all over the country. In her workshops she deals with locating lost animals.

"I have my students work on cases that I'm working on," Carol says. "Some of the animals are not lost, some are on an adventure for themselves. Some are moving on because they have finished teaching that particular family. Some are not going to come home. So it's a matter of learning how to distinguish the difference, and if they are truly lost helping them to find their way back, helping them to tell you where they are."

Carol showed me a letter from a satisfied—in fact, enthusiastic—client, Sylvia Reynaert of Yale, Michigan, of which the following is an excerpt:

Dear Carol,

I want to thank you for communicating with my Belgian Tervern, Chula, a female who never left my farm until one day when she was playing in the field of her home and a gunshot was fired and Chula fled.

When I interviewed Sylvia, she told me:

After notices were posted and local newspaper ads produced no luck in finding Chula, I called Carol Gurney. Carol was able to contact Chula mentally and describe the path she was traveling. She described a covered bridge, an equestrian center, and a major highway that Chula was approaching and that ran along a swampy wooded area.

It took eight days of traveling roads by car and matching the descriptions Carol had received from Chula. On a rainy Sunday out came Chula from the swamp. There was a great reunion, thanks to Carol's ability to read Chula's thoughts.

Another of Carol's clients was Richard Segal of Santa Monica, California. His deaf white cat, Willy, had been lost for two weeks when he called Carol.

"Willy was still alive," Carol reports. "I saw him frozen in one place, because he was too scared to move. I saw him under a house—it looked very clean. Willy told me he could see the wheels of a car off to the left of the house. He also saw a red car, and said there was latticework on the bottom of the house. He told me he had left home because he was upset with the new puppy Richard had brought into the house.

"I explained to Richard that when he went out to look for Willy he needed to be extremely quiet because Willy would be easily frightened. Even though Willy was deaf, his other senses—touch and sight—were so strong that he could perceive keenly.

"Richard had paid everybody he could think of in his neighborhood five dollars to look for his cat—the homeless, the mailmen, the garbage collectors. He circulated five hundred flyers. It was on the night of the Los Angeles riots that he found his cat underneath the house I had described.

"Everything that Willy had described was there: three red cars, latticework on the bottom of the house.

"The street was extremely quiet that night because of a curfew imposed during the riots. Willy was at least one resident of Los Angeles who was happy that night."

———

Patty Breed of Stuart, Florida, says, "I just do animal communication out of curiosity, and I talk with my own animals all the time. I have a horse, two dogs, and a cat. Anybody who asks me, I'll talk with their animals."

When Patty's cat disappeared, she immediately called Phil Roberts in Maine. "It's very hard to contact your own animals," she says. "You're so anxious."

She called her cat K-Marty, because she had found him as a kitten in a Dumpster behind a K mart store.

"I was very distraught when K-Marty disappeared," she said, "so I called Phil. He called me right back and said the cat was fine, he'd be home before morning. While I was on the phone to Phil, I heard a meow. K-Marty had come in the cat door. He was saying, 'I decided to come home early.'"

———————

Raphaela Pope of Berkeley, California, agrees with Phil Roberts that finding lost animals is a toughie.

"A lot of animal communicators don't like to do it," she said, "because it's so hard, and because the results are so uneven."

It also can be quite depressing.

Raphaela recalls, "Once I was doing a consultation on a lost dog and I was just flooded with the sensation of a kind of forlornness, a sadness and confusion. It was very tough. She was an older dog. By the time they called me, she had been on the loose for four or five days, and she was really kind of in extremis. In fact, she did leave the body, she did die. The feeling I got from her was that she was just kind of waiting to die.

"I got little pictures of the area where she was. There was a yard, and a vacant lot at the end of a street. Sometimes these pictures will help a lot; they'll pinpoint a place. Oh yeah, that's the parking lot at the A&P! And other times it's so general that it's not really helpful. We never found the dog. She told us she was leaving the body, and they never found the body. Those are the hardest, where there's not a lot of resolution."

Raphaela has had considerable experience in finding lost animals, but says, "I think it's the area where telepathic communication might be the least helpful. I can't say my finds rate is very high. I wouldn't say more than 20 or 30 percent. But when you do find them it's pretty spectacular. My first was so dramatic that it encouraged me to do many more, in which I have failed miserably on many occasions."

I encouraged Raphaela to tell me about her successes. She told me:

My big success involved a little Manx cat in Arcata (California). They're the ones with no tails. She had an appropriate name—Bobbie. She showed me a picture in which she was in somebody's backyard. She showed me a little garden hut that she was hunkered down in. She also showed me a kind of mad attitude. Her person had just moved, and there were all these people coming and going in their new home. She was not a happy camper. I gave all this information to her person, Christina, and Christina was laughing and crying. "Just like Bobbie," she said. "She's such a prima donna!" Like a lot of cats.

So the next morning I cleared myself out and tried again. There's a lot of emotion around lost animals. People get very upset. The communicator has got to try to keep her objectivity.

So now Bobbie said she had tried to get home that night, but she was still lost. She was crouched down under a parked car. I could see the newspapers blowing around on the ground. The place had a kind of derelict air to it. The most interesting thing was that there were parking meters. I told Christina and she exclaimed, "Parking meters? This is a very small town. There are no parking meters in Arcata!"

But Bobbie had said she didn't think she was very far away.

Well, Christina got in her car to look around, and less than a mile from her new home she was going by a parking lot of the state university, and she noticed there were *PARKING METERS!*

So she leapt out of her car, flew into the parking lot and started calling Bobbie. And Bobbie absolutely appeared! One happy, dirty, hungry cat!

Carol Wright, who lives in Lafayette, a suburb of San Francisco, is a professional animal communicator, but the first animal she ever found was her own cat, Lucy. A voice just came to her—it was Lucy's.

"Actually," Carol told me, "Lucy started me with animal communication. I was sitting on my couch watching TV with a friend, and all of a sudden I heard Lucy say she was lost. I looked around, and sure enough, she was gone. That was the first time she had ever been missing. When she wasn't in the house, she always stayed in the yard.

"It was the oddest thing. It was just a thought that all of a sudden was in my head, and I knew it didn't come from me. It was very weird. It's not weird to me now, but when you're not expecting it and it's just sort of out of the blue it's rather unsettling. And then when it turns out to be true it's even more startling. It's kind of like a thought that's in your head but doesn't come from inside of you."

Carol, who at that time lived in Houston, Texas, had heard of animal communication but didn't know any practitioners of the art. So she called New Age bookstores and other likely places and came up with the name of Griffin Kanter, who then lived in Katy, a suburb of Houston.

"Griffin told me how to bring Lucy home mentally," Carol told me, "and she came home the next day."

I had already interviewed Griffin, who now lives in Houston, about various aspects of her career as a communicator, but hadn't touched on finding lost animals. I wanted to find out how she did this, and checked back with her.

"It was something my cat Casey taught me," she said. "He had disappeared for about five days. During that time, when I was home, I would keep calling him, saying, 'Come home, Casey, come home,' so that he could focus on my energy and make it back. I was talking to him regularly when he was gone. I lived out in the suburbs on the west side of Houston, and a lot of it is undeveloped pasture land. All Casey could tell me was that he was crossing pastures and that the sun was behind him when it set, so he was coming from the west, which wasn't enough for me to go and pick him up.

"When he came home, five days later, I sat down with him and talked with him about what had happened. He said that my calling had set up a beacon of light, and all he had to do was aim toward that light. When Carol called, she knew that her cat Lucy was near, but that was as far as she could get because of her own emotions. So I said, 'Why don't you put up a white light around your house, and put up a beacon that will keep flashing THIS IS HOME and then visualize Lucy coming home. And keep calling her.' That information helped her to put up the right visual, which Lucy was able to link into."

I asked Griffin and Carol if they do much in the way of looking for lost animals. Neither does. Griffin told me, "I don't do a lot of lost pets, because I don't feel that is my strength. I can get a picture of where they are initially. I can see around them, and I can talk to them. But I can't get them if they move. There is an element of tracking that lost-animal communicators have to do that I don't seem quite to have."

Carol said, "I don't do lost animals because it's very difficult. We don't see things the same way an animal does."

As Phil Roberts said, "It's a toughie."

Despite the difficulty, Tim Beihoff, an animal communicator in Sussex, Wisconsin, has been drawn to seeking lost animals and has done a lot of it. Tim is one of the few male communicators I found. I asked him why the percentage of male communicators is so small, and he replied, "I guess with most men it doesn't fit the macho image. If men realize they can do this, they don't necessarily talk about it. But I don't have a problem with that. In any case, people are opening up more and more all the time—men and women."

Tim, a man in his early thirties, studied police science in college. "I was going to be a cop," he said. "I still have a full-time job; I'm a salesman. But my hobby is that I show dogs, both my own dogs and for other people. I'm very close to the animals. Because of the amount of time I was spending on dog shows I got out of police science.

"When I first became aware of animal communication, I was a fencesitter. You were going to have to prove it to me. But now I'm in the middle of the field with the rest of the crazies."

Tim feels that telepathic contact—with animals, humans, whomever or whatever—is something that we all experience but just don't notice. He says he only became aware that he was using telepathy a few years ago, and then it was with people, not animals. As he told me:

For me things happened very quickly. The first thing of this sort I remember is a friend calling me on my answering machine, saying she wouldn't be able to call me later in the evening because she was going out to look for her sister. I didn't get this message until several hours later. But in the meantime, I was flashed pictures of her sitting in a bar with her sister. I got colors, the number of drinks they'd had, the positions in which they were sitting, a lamp on the table between them. And this was a woman who doesn't drink much, who doesn't do bars. I talked with her the next day and found out that at the very time I was seeing this stuff that it was literally correct. That was in August of '93. It was the first time I really noticed.

Once you notice it, you look at it from a different angle. You pay attention. I started getting little flashes from one of my own dogs. For most of us who do this, communicating with your own animals is usually very difficult. Because you know them so well, you think, is this something I would have said? I was totally green at all this. I still have a difficult time with any animal when he's sitting right in front of me, it's too distracting.

Distance doesn't matter in all of this. I found two lost cats in Prague, Czechoslovakia, and everything worked out just as I said it would.

I tend to see quite a bit around the animal. Missing animals are difficult to do. It's hard to keep your emotions out of it. I get very personally involved. Sometimes I tend to sort of see through the animal's eyes, I see what's around them, whatever they want to show me. Most of the time it's in pictures. Sometimes I smell things. Sometimes it's just a feeling. I have the owners give me the animal's name, their own name, where they live, and what the animal looks like—colors, and so on. You have to try to be certain that you're not getting the wrong animal—another one with that name and that general description. You get a lot of your connection through the owner. You're getting their emotions. So when you ask for Sparky, you probably get the right animal because you've got the owner right there, the connection. Usually after the first contact with the owner, or somebody very close to the animal, I can then talk to the animal on my own.

One of the more memorable cases for me was a stolen malamute-wolf mix in Santa Fe, New Mexico. The dog's name was Spirit. He had been gone for several months. When they contacted me, I was able to describe the person who had stolen him, and it turned out to be correct. I described his owner, and was correct.

I was almost literally on the dog's trail for two months. He was showing me he was in kind of a small, dark house. They kept telling me they have these adobe houses down there. I said it felt to me like it was a mobile home. We found out later, when the dog was recovered, that it was in fact a mobile home, where the guy who had stolen the dog was living at the time. The dog eventually got away from that guy. The guy came forward, that's how we verified my description of him. He wanted to help find the dog.

I felt that the dog was now with a woman who had some children. I was even getting directions. This was a dog I'd never met, a place I'd never been to. It took a while, but they ended up finding the dog, and he had been in the places I said.

I was down in Santa Fe just a few weeks ago, and I met Spirit. Most of these lost or stolen animals are never found, but this was one that was, and I got to meet him.

I asked Tim if his efforts had had a direct influence in the recovery of Spirit.

"I guess so," he said. "They kept following the directions that I got, the descriptions of houses and people and areas. They put up posters in those areas. Somebody from the electric company had seen the dog and then saw the poster and called the owner."

————————

Another stolen-animal case that Tim worked on involved a cat in Chicago. Tim told me:

He had been gone several months. As it turned out, there again I described the man involved with stealing him. I described a house, right down to the colors of the house. It didn't sound right to the owner of the cat. She said there just weren't houses like that in Chicago, with a porch or deck or whatever in front of the house.

I also got that the people who stole the cat felt they could do better by this cat. It was an extremely overweight cat, an indoor cat. They felt that the owner was killing the cat with kindness. I told the owner, "They've put the cat on a diet. They know that you're looking for him, they've seen the posters. But they're not going to return him, because they think they can do better."

I also told her that she was going to get law enforcement involved at some point, and since she had a lot of good information going for her she probably would recover her cat. And just two weeks ago I got a message on my machine that she had in fact got law enforcement involved, that my description of the guy who stole the cat was correct, and that he had put the cat on a diet. And that the cat was now home with her.

It really does you good to get validation that way. But I don't know if I'm going to continue to do communications for stolen animals. It's just so hard, the owners are so emotional. You get involved, and *you* get emotional. And many times they do not come back.

Other kinds of cases are more fun to do, because there isn't the stress of emotion. A person will call you and ask you to work with her cat because the cat won't use the litter box. You speak with the animal, and they call you back a week or so later and are so happy, because now they have done what the cat had asked for and the cat is now using the litter box.

Animals have their own opinions on things. There's probably a reason why they're not using the litter box. Maybe the owners don't clean it enough. I had one case where the woman put it on top of a washing machine, and the cat was an older cat. It was too hard to jump up there. I didn't know she had put it up there, and the cat told me it was up so high. I told the woman, "The cat wants you to put the litter box down where it's easier for him to get at it; he'll use it then." And he did.

Tim also recounted to me his efforts in a law enforcement case down in Houston. He told me:

At the time, they thought a dog was the only witness. It was a murder. I think there was also a human witness. The detective called me, and also a brother of the victim. Through the dog, I described all kinds of things that they already knew were factual, things I had no way of knowing. They were kind of tight-lipped about giving me validation; they tested me a lot. For example, they asked what was the body wrapped in. I told them some type of heavy material, like a section of carpet, or a throw rug. It turned out that it was a carpet. They asked me where the body was dumped, and I said there was a lot of junk around. It turned out to be a dump.

They were looking for a weapon, a gun. One communicator had told them it was buried under cement at the airport, where the victim's truck had been found. I didn't get that at all. I kept getting that it was under water. At the time, I didn't know this was in Houston, I just knew it was in Texas. So I asked Adele Tate and other friends who do this, without giving them too much information, and they all said it was under water. They said the water was not in ditches, but was big enough to be a lake. Then I found that this happened right on the Gulf of Mexico. So I felt that that was where the gun was, and that they were never going to find it.

I asked Tim how all this was related to animal communication.

"Because of the dog," he said. "The original purpose was to talk to the dog. They wanted a description of the person who did the killing. They've arrested the same guy twice for it, and I do think they have the right person. But I saw some things connected with this case that the dog could not have seen, but that the victim would have seen. I told them things that were correct, like where he was shot, how many times he was shot, things that the dog wouldn't know."

Detective stories often confuse me, although I love them, and Tim's account was starting to spin my head a bit. "Do you mean," I asked him, "that the only two witnesses would have been the dog and the man who was killed?"

"Those are the two I worked with," he replied, "but I do believe there was a third witness. That person didn't want me to see who it was, so I always saw him from behind. It might even have been a woman."

I asked Tim, "Did you know from the dog that there was another witness?"

"It could have been that," he replied, "or wherever else this was coming from."

"Are you saying that you were able to contact the person who was shot, who is in spirit now, and that he was telling you these things?" I asked.

"I believe so," Tim said.

"Do you do that very often, contact people who are no longer alive?" I asked.

"No," he said, "but I do with animals. It's really no different after they've transitioned. In fact, sometimes it's easier that way. Sometimes I tell things to their owners that only their owners would know, and it just blows their owners' minds away. With animals, one of the things that makes them so much fun, and in a sense easier, is that they are honest. It's pretty much black and white; they don't have an agenda. They'll tell you the truth generally, although they'll tell you only what they want you to know. You try to do this with the spirits of humans and they'll tell you it's this and they'll tell you it's that, just like they would if they were alive and right there speaking to you. People can be quite devious, but animals are very honest."

———————

Laura Simpson was born and brought up—fourth generation—in Fairfield, Iowa, a town of 9,700 in the southeastern corner of the state. Except for college years at the University of Wisconsin, she has spent

Laura Simpson with Albert; photo by Rick Donhauser

almost all of her life in Fairfield. She's old family. But she isn't exactly the sort of person you'd expect to find out there where the corn is as high as an elephant's eye. In fact, for New Age hipness she'd fit in perfectly in Greenwich Village or Berkeley.

Laura seems to have been a practicing psychic from day one of her life. She says, "My mother recognized early on that I had the ability to talk to and hear animals. She could do that, too, so she helped foster it in me. My grandmother was also psychic and was very supportive and nurturing of my ability."

Her father was a lawyer, and tended to be more left-brain, involved with the mundane matters of this world. What a life he must have led with those three exotic women!

Laura majored in early childhood education in college and returned to Fairfield as a social worker. In her job she was often called on to testify in child abuse cases. "It was very draining work," she says.

After some years, she searched for more congenial employment, and became secretary to a well-known psychic. Before long, the psychic was telling Laura that she should be doing the same thing. "She pretty much pushed me to hang out my own shingle," Laura says. Laura gave it some thought, and decided she didn't want to deal only with people. "I feel that animals need a voice," she says. And since her social work job had constantly exposed her to the less wholesome side of human nature, animals would be refreshing. "People have so much convoluted junk on them," she said. "Animals are pretty much straightforward."

She told me that she found eight of the first ten lost animals she worked on, which is quite extraordinary. "I'm the one," she said, "that other animal communicators refer people to, because my success rate is about 80 percent."

And indeed a couple of well-known animal communicators mentioned to me spontaneously that Laura was definitely somebody I ought to contact if I were writing about finding lost animals.

Laura feels that her time in human services has helped her. "Because of all the crisis work I've done with people," she says, "I can handle the human emotions of it and cut through to what's going on with the animals."

I asked Laura the obligatory questions about her background. Married? With children? I love her answer: "No, I've never married. I came close five times, but by the time the guys would ask me I'd be so sick of their stuff that there's no way I'd want to sign up for it. I think that in not being married it's allowed me to be spiritual if I want. I don't have children, but I've always taken care of everybody else's children."

I've gone into such detail about the down-home aspects of Laura's life on this planet because when we got into the nitty-gritty of her conversations with animals some of her observations might be a bit difficult for a general audience to accept. Although, dear reader, if you've gotten this far you may have developed some calluses on your doubt muscles.

"The first thing a person needs to do if their pet is lost," Laura told me, "is to take some Rescue Remedy. It's a Bach flower essence. If Bach is not available, they can take a preparation made by a company called Ellon. It's the same thing, and it's called the Calming Essence. If you're wigged out or under stress it takes the edges off."

[I might mention that a couple of years ago in Florida I was strenuously stressed and markedly wigged out, and I tried some Rescue Remedy. I wasn't aware of any change in my condition, but I guess I'm hard to rescue.]

As Laura was saying:

If you're wigged out, you're not really helping the pet or yourself. Because the pet tries to keep in touch with you through telepathy, and if all they're picking up are your emotions, the whole fear scenario that you're manifesting, it's not helpful. You want to stay grounded and calm.

I think it's important for people to learn that they can trust themselves. If they meditate, that's a good thing too. Surround the pet with white light, and themselves with white light. And from the pet's little belly button and the person's belly button, the person needs to pull out a little imaginary string of white light, and then tie a knot. That will help bring the pet back to them. Throughout the day, it's a good idea to go into silence and check that string of white light, to see if the knot is still tied.

People need to trust their intuition. We humans tend to rationalize everything. We have to decide if it's really logical or not. You need to trust that little soft voice. It speaks very softly, and it speaks only once, because the logic starts yelling over it.

And if you're not getting any results—right away call an animal communicator who specializes in finding lost pets.

———————

I asked Laura to tell me of some specific experiences she has had in practicing her specialty. She responded with a couple of cases, both of which involve observations that the reader can take or leave. I tend to take them, but then I was loving Laura's personality and her slant on this wacky life we're all tied into. Here's what she said:

I had one guy out in Vermont, Bill Crain, who's a DNR guy. He works for the Department of Natural Resources, in a state park. He'd never done anything esoteric before. He had lost his dog, Cashew, a German shorthair. He called me up in a panic. I told him to get some Rescue Remedy, and it really helped a lot. Even if the pet's person is working with a communicator, it helps if he is calm.

I went into meditation and checked in with the dog, and I found out what the dog's and the person's soul contract was. Their contract was about rescuing each other. Through lifetimes, they had created these crisis dynamics, so they could pay each other back for being rescued from the time before. So I asked permission from God and Jesus if the contract could be rewritten. And I checked in with the higher selves of Bill Crain and Cashew to see if they wanted it to be rewritten. And they both said yes, they were tired of that dynamic in their relationship. The new contract would be that they would always be there for each other.

So that took a lot of the stress off Cashew's being off somewhere, although he stayed missing for another week or ten days. Then I got telepathically that he had gone to a farm that was close to the park. Bill had sent me a topographic map of the park. I told him what area the farm was in, and he began stopping at farmhouses. He found an older couple who had taken Cashew in, and they were reunited.

———————

"Sometimes," Laura told me, "pets take off because there's creepy stuff in the house. Sometimes entities, ghosts—whatever you want to call them—get attracted to people or pets. And pets tend to see ghosts easier than we do, so a ghost will tend to hang around a pet more because the ghost can get the pet's attention. It's something to play with. I had a case like that in Fairfield."

Fascinated, I told Laura to tell me about the Fairfield case. This is what she said:

A little sheltie always stuck with her people, but this day she was with them visiting a farm where some friends lived and she ran off and they couldn't get her back. They asked me to help, and what I got was that the sheltie had taken on the ghost of a deer who had been killed on the highway. When animals get hit on a road, half the time they don't know what has happened. They don't know they are supposed to go into the white light, the higher spiritual planes. It's the same with people who are killed suddenly. So they're just hanging around. This little sheltie had picked up the deer entity as the family was driving by in their car. The deer had just been killed on the road. The sheltie's mistress said the dog had looked out the window as the car passed the dead deer on the road, and the dog's behavior had immediately started changing. The deer entity had pretty much taken over the whole thought processes of the dog.

I mentioned to Laura that for me this had a familiar ring. In writing books on ghosts, I had run across cases of people who had been killed on the road and who had reportedly become ghostly hitchhikers. Sometimes, according to accounts I got, drivers would pick up seemingly living passengers who would then disappear in unorthodox ways. One in South Africa disappeared from the backseat of a motorcycle.

Laura responded, "Yeah, I've had people get in the car with me when I go out to the cemetery. I clear them off—I ask God to please send an angel to come and take these souls into the light. What happens typically, if an entity takes on an animal, is that the animal's energy starts to drain. The animal's physical energy is going to support something that doesn't have a body. This little sheltie was out running around in the woods with the ghost of the deer. Searchers kept tracking the dog's paws with live deer whom the dead deer was running with."

Laura mentioned that she connected with the sheltie by the use of Reiki, an energy discipline.

"And then," she said, "I lifted the spirit of the deer and sent him to the light. I told the family that they would find the dog in the corner of a field near the road, and within half an hour a lady in a car saw the dog. She had heard on the radio that the dog was missing, and she got the dog into her car and brought it home to its family."

"Often," Laura said, "an animal will leave its home to resolve some spiritual problem. Typically, pets come to us to help us with our spiritual evolution. It's all part of their contract with humanity. Sometimes it's for spiritual reasons, and oftentimes they take on some emotional problem we're having. Or they'll take on some physical problem, like the person may have contracted cancer or diabetes or something, and the pet takes it on.

"I have an older lady who takes thyroid medication, and all of a sudden her dog had to take thyroid medication. She was told she needed more fiber in her diet, and all of a sudden she was told that her dog needed more fiber in *his* diet. I think what is happening is that the dog is taking on part of the lady's burden so that she doesn't get hit with her physical problems so badly."

Throughout my interviews with communicators, this concept kept coming up. I've put it into this book at various places, both earlier in this chapter and elsewhere. The following quotation is from communicator Kate Reilly of Shelby, North Carolina:

> Very often the animal will be expressing the exact same disease as its owner, and taking it on to help the person. Animals are present in our lives to be our teachers, our guides, and our healers. That's one of the ways that they heal us, they take on the person's tension. Very often the animal will take on something like colitis, or it may be back pain.

I told Kate about a case Nancy Regalmuto had encountered, which I relate in more detail in Chapter 5, in which a horse had declined into a dangerously ill condition. Nancy found that he had been taking on the depression of his teenage owner.

"It happens all the time," Kate said.

Morgan Jurdan and friend; photo by Marcie A. Bomarito

Another idea that Laura Simpson expressed that came up repeatedly in my interviews with other communicators was that many animals are more than they appear to be, that they are spiritual guides to the humans they are with. Morgan Jurdan of Amboy, Washington, has been doing animal communication professionally for only four years, but she told me that she has spoken with animals since she was a child. She has taken courses from Penelope Smith and now teaches workshops herself. She said:

When I took my first class, I asked various animals there what their purpose in life was. Some dogs and cats just liked being dogs and cats, they liked the connection to people, they liked being in that kind of body. Others are spiritual helpers. One dog said he was a spirit guide. I asked him what lesson he had for me, and he said, "You know that problem you were having last year?" I was going through an emotional growth issue at that time. The dog actually told me what the issue was, and gave me ideas on finding a solution. I was just blown away because I had just met this dog, so how could he know me and know I'd gone through this?

It let me open up to the fact that we're all connected on the grand scale, people and animals and everything else. He was the dog of a participant in the class. He was a yellow Lab, and he had a red hand-kerchief around his head. On the second day you bring your own pet, and then we all communicate with all the animals. This particular dog told me that his purpose was to be a spirit guide to three different people, the person he lived with and two others.

A lot of animals who live with us are with us for a purpose—most of them are. But they are individuals. Some are just here to cheer us up. Some are like teachers, or gurus. They are teachers to us in countless ways.

We had a dog named Duke. Duke had this game he played with us. If we threw him a ball he would not bring it back to us. He wants us to chase him, that's his game. You've got to chase him around the house and catch him and then actually take it out of his mouth. So a little child of three who lived in a trailer near our house came around and he threw the ball to Duke, and Duke came up to him and dropped it right at his feet, and sat there. I was amazed, and so was the boy's mother, because she knew of Duke's usual game with balls. She goes, "My little boy was mauled by a dog; he's never gone up to another dog in his life. He's scared to death of dogs."

And we watched those two play for fifteen minutes. The dog did it again and again. The dog was being uncharacteristic, and the child was too, but I could sense the communication. The dog had told the little boy that it was safe, and the boy knew he was safe with this dog. We sat and watched them, speechless, at this wonderful dance of love, with the child communicating with the dog and the dog communicating with the child. We had tears in our eyes.

13

Communicating with Wild Animals, Trees, Bushes, Slugs, and the Occasional Rock

I n the 1970s a quaint custom involving rocks surfaced—the pet rock fad. If it didn't exactly sweep the country, at least it trickled across it. I was the editor of a magazine in New England at the time, and I thought it would be terminally cute to run a rock on the cover. A fellow named Bob Cudmore, host of a local radio talk show, had a rock that he claimed to set great store by. So Bob appeared in the magazine, holding the rock on a leash, along with a couple of little girls who also had rocks on leashes.

Little did I know that some twenty years hence, as the century was getting ready to turn, thousands of people would be taking relationships with rocks quite seriously, not as the joke we thought of it back in the seventies. And these people would be well-educated, accomplished people, possessors of tickets that are respected in our bread and butter, mundane society.

An example is Kate Solisti, a professional animal communicator based in Santa Fe, New Mexico. Kate is a 1980 graduate of Smith College. She grew up in a conventional family in New Jersey. "I'm the black sheep of the family," she chuckles, "although my mother deals with it quite well; she even tells her friends what I do.

Bob Cudmore and two fellow rock lovers, with their pet rocks on leashes; photo by Berkshire Sampler

"I was born with the ability to hear animals and plants," she says, "but I shut it down as a child when I was about eight. But after college, the desire to connect with the planet was bubbling up." She took a position with an environmental organization in Washington, D.C.

Kate Solisti and William; photo by Carolyn Wright

"I had blocked out a lot of the memories of my childhood involving trees, wild animals, rocks. A lot of things have come back to me as I've worked to heal that part of me that was blocked. It was the trees that began speaking to me when I first began coming back into being able to hear."

She began spending time in a small park in Washington. "There was a particular rock that I loved to sit on," she relates. "I called it the Grandmother Rock, because it felt very loving to me. Somehow, it had a real feminine nature. When I sat on that rock, I felt very accepted, very safe."

At one point, she told me, she heard laughing. There was no one around, and she realized it was the essence, or whatever, of the rock that she was hearing.

"I asked, 'What's so funny?'" Kate told me. "And the rock said, 'Human beings are so funny. They race around like crazy, and they miss almost everything.' I laughed when I heard that. I said, 'I think you're right.'"

But prior to Kate's first conversation with the rock, there was the tree. As Kate put it:

One day I was sitting on the Grandmother Rock, being quiet and listening to the sounds of the woods, and I heard—it wasn't a voice, but
a thought dropped into my mind—"Come on over here."

I looked around and asked, "Who said that?"

It was almost as though my eyes were magnetized toward this little
tree. It wasn't a remarkable tree, it wasn't extraordinarily big or beautiful, it was just one of many trees in this little wooded area.

I said, "Tree, did you say that to me?"

It began to kind of glow. There was an extraordinary sense of
energy in this tree. It was as if I all of a sudden became part of the
tree, because I could feel the energy coming up from the earth, I could
feel it sort of reaching up to the sky, a tremendous amount of energy
going through this tree.

And at the same time it said, "We're paying attention to you."

I said, "You are?"

And it said, "Yes, we are, and you're doing quite well."

I was just overjoyed; I couldn't get over it. Then I thought, "Oh
my God, am I losing it? What's happening here?" I remembered
from my childhood my cat talking to me, and other animals, but
not trees, so this was a bit of a shock. I began to delve into Native
American stuff, because that was the only reference I had of any
kind of conversation with plants or trees. I didn't tell anybody, not
even my husband.

Afterward, I would go to the woods, particularly when I was feeling
depressed, and ask the tree to talk to me. Nothing would happen,
which was terribly frustrating. But it was a very good lesson, because
what I learned was that I was needing it too much. I was pulling too
hard. I was actually pushing them away. I was creating my own block
to receiving, because I was pushing the energy out.

I had to learn that the times I could hear the trees were when I
was the most calm and centered, when I wasn't frazzled, when I wasn't
tired, I wasn't stressed, I wasn't angry. If there were powerful emotions happening to me, I couldn't hear the trees. When I teach, I help
people learn how to quiet their minds. The mind is so busy. How can
you hear anything when you're talking all the time?

I suggested in the Preface to this book that some of the concepts herein might be a bit hard to accept, so it might be a good move to put your disbeliever on hold. In this particular chapter, the idea that trees have consciousness and can communicate might be considered the most offbeat of the offbeat. But rocks? I suppose you could call that the most offbeat of the offbeat squared, or offbeat to the third power.

When I finished writing this chapter I read it to a friend, David Fine, a retired businessman whom I sometimes use as a litmus test. He managed to get by the trees, but boggled on the rocks. Rocks, he insisted, have no consciousness. And that's that! The next day, I came across what struck me as a nicely written rebuttal to my friend's point of view, in a book by Machaelle Small Wright entitled *Behaving as if the God in All Life Mattered*. Machaelle is cofounder of Perelanda, a Findhorn-like nature research center in Jeffersonton, Virginia. She had this to say in her book:

> I have a friend who likes to refer to numb people—extraordinarily dense people—as people who have the consciousness of a rock. Cute, but wrong. The density of the Mineral Kingdom refers to its power, not to a "disconnectedness" from life. Minerals bridge time. They use the same form for centuries, even eons, and when we touch into the intelligence it's quite possible for us to experience a particular historical period or event that is contained within the "memory bank" of this specific mineral. An example: A woman in one of my workshops chose to get in touch with the consciousness of a stone she had picked up on a beach in Ireland. What happened during the meditation was that the stone gave her a gift—a gift of joy. To do this, it flashed the woman into an idyllic beach scene where many children were playing and having a wonderful time and the woman was enveloped with a sensation of joy which she received from the stone. But the scene wasn't contemporary. It was actually a scene that had occurred in the late 1800s on a beach in Holland—which was where this stone was sitting until being washed to the shores of Ireland. (p. 110)

I became very conscious during my research for this book that a high percentage of communicators with animals and nature have a common history—they had unhappy childhoods. In fact, I feel that I myself had

as unhappy a childhood as the next braggart. Maybe that's why I write
so many books about other dimensions—I've never much liked this one.

Two people in particular expressed this aspect of the spiritual life—
the communicative life—in language so full of meaning and feeling that
it was poetic. They are Denise Kinch of Groveland, Massachusetts, and
Nancy Regalmuto of New York City and Long Island.

Denise said:

As a child, very often I was told that animals and birds and trees can't
talk to me. I shut it down for a while because of my upbringing. But
I always spent much time with animals and in the woods, much more
time than with people. Nature has always been my saving grace. My

Denise Kinch

parents always called me a renegade, because I always fought the system; I always questioned why. I was brought up in Catholic schools. That was their life, and that's great, but it wasn't who I was. My brother and sister were the perfect son, the perfect daughter. And I was in the middle. I never wore dresses; I climbed trees. I was with animals more than people. I just wasn't what my parents wanted, and I created my own disharmony in the family by being that. I was always unworthy of them; I could never get their love. They were never pleased with who I was, and I was never pleased with who I was. But I knew there was more out there, so I kept searching and searching.

My husband is a CPA, the controller in an insurance company. Very heavy left-brain, but he puts up with me. He drives a motorcycle too, so he's all right. My children are very open to communication, they see more than I see, they hear more than I hear. They have never been shut down, they have never been told the animals don't talk. But in most of our culture, the shutdown comes right from birth. You're told you can't walk with nature.

Well, I've always walked with nature. I see trees' auras, they just dance. When I was raking leaves this morning, I was watching the trees with their brilliant colors around them. If you talk to the stone people, you can *be* them, you can *feel* them. They have so much knowledge, so much power, because they have been there forever, they have been here before the trees. They have so much to give us.

There's so much violence and anger and torment and abuse and sadness and injustice in the world, but if you look at the broad spectrum you'll see that something is changing. I think the world is changing for the better. People think that the world is about to end, but I think it's only going to end as we know it within ourselves, rather than on a physical level. I think we're becoming more energy-bodied, we're transforming our own bodies and minds.

Nancy Regalmuto is a world-class psychic, a clairvoyant who can go at will into other dimensions, who can perform extraordinary feats of mysticism. I have known her for several years and have been witness to some of those feats. Some are as mundane as knowing which racehorses or sports teams are going to win. For several years, Nancy wrote

Nancy Regalmuto

a prediction column for *Metro Turf*, a publication of the *Daily Racing Form*. It was so startlingly accurate that the editors couched it in the form of riddles, such as: "The trainer's wife, Vera, will be pleased." Nancy was a professional gambler for a time. But her real vocation is helping animals and people with their emotional and physical difficulties.

As a child, she had the problems that a very young psychic person is heiress to. At school one day she caused a furor when she kept jumping up and insisting that something must be done, that the president was going to be killed. When she refused to be quiet, she was sent to the principal's office. That afternoon, John F. Kennedy was assassinated.

"It came over the loudspeaker," Nancy recalls, "that the president had just been shot. The teacher was looking at me, everybody was looking at me. We were all told to go home. Nobody said anything to me—they just looked at me as though I were weird. I didn't understand it. They acted as though I had done something bad, and I couldn't grasp that I had."

Nancy had already had traumatic experiences. For starters, nobody understood her. But one particular experience played a large part in turning her away from humankind, and toward nature. As she told me:

I was about five and my best friend was Stevie, about the same age. We had a turtle we had found. We raised it. We did everything for that turtle. We fed it and washed it. We made a little tunnel for him. We took him everywhere. He was like our prize possession, we loved him dearly. This went on for about six months. He was our pet.

So one day our next-door neighbor, Jimmy—he was about thirteen—was outside building something. He looked over the hedge between our houses and said, "Oh, let me see your turtle."

Stevie and I were like proud parents of our turtle, you know. The turtle, it seemed to me, was a little reluctant to go to Jimmy, but I thought it's OK. So I gave the turtle to Jimmy, and he was petting it. There was this tree stump, and he put the turtle on this stump. We were on the other side of the hedge, watching. Then all of a sudden, from behind the other side of the stump, Jimmy lifted up a hammer and crushed the turtle right in front of us. Smashed him. There was blood everywhere. I couldn't believe it. I felt at that point, you can't trust humans. And I felt guilty, because the turtle had seemed like he didn't want to go to Jimmy, and I let him, I handed him over. I felt you can't trust humans; humans are cruel. It was a horrible, horrible thing to see as a very young child. All of a sudden somebody betrays you and hurts you to that degree.

These kinds of things really shut me off from human life. I became very silent, very quiet, very into myself. I began to become an absorber of all living things. I learned to keep my mouth shut. I didn't say much, growing up. I basically stopped interrelating in the human world; I shut down.

And as I became more quiet, I learned to hear things, things that other people didn't get to hear because they were so busy talking, they were too busy thinking. I would go for a walk and I'd sit out in the fields and my quietness would draw to me the voices of the unseen, unheard world. And I began to have other experiences. Beings came to me to keep me company, for companionship, to be my friends and to guide me. To teach me about myself.

God comes to you when you're still, when you're very still. When you're moving about you're moving too much for Him to come to you. Not only moving physically. Sometimes people come to me for help. They say, "I've been here and I've been there, I've been all over, but nothing helps me." I reply, "Why don't you just stay still for a little while? Stop seeking for a moment. Stay still in one place, go on retreat and just pray. No outside communications, no TV, no radio, no telephone calls, no people. Just silence and stillness, and allow God to come to you."

Be like a chameleon. A reptile goes into a hibernating mode. He sits on a tree. And his color becomes as the tree. He becomes the vibration of the tree. He turns into a part of the tree. In that moment, he has become very receptive to everything around him, because now he is perfectly still, and now he has become part of something else. When I was a child I learned how to become chameleonlike, to be next to a tree and imitate the vibration of the tree. I would make myself like the thing I was trying to communicate with, so that I would understand. I would change my energy pattern into that of a tree. I would be silent and go within and try to feel with all my senses what that tree was like. I would imitate its vibrations inside of myself, I would become like the tree, and I could hear it.

Adele Tate of Byron, Illinois, usually works with animals, but while taking a course from Linda Tellington-Jones she learned that trees are also well worth talking to.

Linda Tellington-Jones is an internationally famed healer of animals who has designed treatment that she calls the Tellington TTouch. She developed her method from her studies with Moshe Feldenkrais, who originated techniques of movement aimed at helping people reach higher physical, emotional, and intellectual potentials. Tellington-Jones, who is based in Santa Fe, adapted many of these methods for use with animals.

"I learned to hug trees in Linda's course," Adele told me. "She said: 'OK, this afternoon we're going to go out and talk to the trees.'

"I thought, Did she just say we're going to talk to trees? Yeah, right. But people began getting some amazing results. On that day, I got a one-word response from each side of the tree I picked."

"What sort of responses?" I asked.

"The first question I asked was 'Who am I?' And the tree said, 'Old.'"

"You heard this voice in your head?" I asked.

"Yeah . . . but no . . . well, yeah. But it was not my chatter voice. I heard a man's voice, and that's what convinced me. It was very gruff, but it wasn't angry."

"What kind of tree was it?" I asked.

"It was a very old oak tree, and I loved it. I thought, Wow, there's my tree!"

"Did you put your arms around it?" I asked.

She laughed. "Yes. You hold the tree so your heart is right next to it."

I had a confession to make. When I started working on this book, I began doing a bit of tree hugging myself. I was trying to get into the spirit of the thing. With my analytical mind, there were no results, of course. I told Adele, "There's a beautiful public path right next to where I live, and there are great trees all along it. But there's always some jogger or hiker or cycler coming along, so I tend to lean my back against the tree so they won't think I'm crazy."

"Yeah, see?" Adele replied. "We're thinking about other things rather than getting into the tree."

She told me about her own private tree at her home, which she calls the Grandmother Tree. "That's why my Grandmother Tree is so perfect," she said, "because nobody can see us. I sleep down there, I sit there and I climb in her branches. You just feel the vibrations of the tree. Just ask to feel it, you can feel it. It expands and contracts. And you can feel the motion of the tree. No matter how big it is, you can feel it waving."

"What else did the first tree you hugged say?" I asked.

Adele replied, "I asked, 'Why have I come here?' And he said, 'Animals.' I asked, 'Where am I going?' And he said, 'Universe.' I asked, 'Where did I come from?' And he said, 'Away.'"

I wanted to know more about Adele's special tree at her home. "What are some of the experiences you've had with your Grandmother Tree?" I asked. "Why do you call it your Grandmother Tree?" She answered:

It's a huge tree, and right next to it a smaller tree came up. Two branches from the smaller tree have wrapped themselves around the big tree, as though they're hugging it. And there are seven other trees in a row, in front of the big tree. I said once that she was like a mother tree.

"Not a mother tree," she said, "a grandmother tree."

One time she told me to lie down and meditate with her. She took me inside. She told me that my body was in her nucleus, right below the surface of the ground. She took me down into the roots. I could smell the dirt, I could feel the coolness and the darkness. Then I surged up through the trunk of the tree into the branches. I could feel the waving back and forth. Then she brought me back down again, and I was like a fetus there at the base, feeling the pulsating of the nutrition from the mother.

I told Adele I was going to make another effort to communicate with the trees that border the path near my home.

"Yeah," she said, "go ahead and put your back against the tree if you want. Just be taken away with it, let yourself go, just become the tree and let your mind go into a meditative state with it."

Laura Silva lives in Petersham, Massachusetts, about thirty miles from me, and I have been aware of her mysticism for some years. Her organic garden is something of a legend in these parts. She grows things that almost nobody else in this northern clime does, such as melons. Damage from wildlife is minimal in her garden, compared with the gardens of her neighbors, where deer and other animals come and eat up a storm. She told me, "The wildlife doesn't forage on my land because of my working with them."

Laura holds a master's degree in psychology and has been in clinical practice for more than ten years. When I asked if I should refer to her as a practicing psychologist, she laughed and said, "I'd call myself more a shamanic transpersonal psychotherapist."

She has studied with Buddhist teachers, with shamans, with American Indians. "I've worked," she says, "with great teachers of the East and West to help me remember what I always knew about the self and soul, about other realms."

Laura was an only child, and lived out in the country. She told me:

I felt very alone, and in a way very different. I was always surrounded by nature. I was in contact with wild creatures, as well as domesticated animals. For me, there never was a distinction between nature

Laura Silva

and me. I always had that point of consciousness available. I was always open, just as animals have that natural ability to pass through worlds—of being in our world and also being able to pass through and be open to other worlds.

I never lost that, there never was a division or separateness, which usually happens when we become older and acculturated and educated. I have retained the ability to just slip into nature and communicate, in a nonverbal way, telepathically.

My mother was open to my psychic abilities, there was a matriarchal lineage. My grandmother from Italy had tremendous psychic ability, and I was exposed to that when I was very young. But my relationship with people was always very difficult, because I had this gift where I would be able to just feel into animals, trees, plants, and so forth. Most people would never talk about that, so I would feel very different.

I would go into the woods, to hidden places, or I would climb a particular tree. In those places, I would completely move out of our realm, and open into communing with the tree, into that feeling of intuitive consciousness. I was able to blend into the tree, to hear what the tree was saying. I would be able to know certain animals were there before they came out and made their presence known. They could be wild animals—rabbits, turtles. I would befriend them. They would be my friends. So I had these wild places I would go to, and trees I would climb. These were like my teachers, these were my friends.

I asked Laura what the trees would say to her.

"It would always be a message of great comfort," she replied. "You're fine, you're OK, you're loved, we love you, you're special, you're wonderful. It would be a great comfort, and it would also be a feeling that we were connected even though we had different forms, that we had known each other before. Whether a tree or a bush or an animal, the message was that we were vibrationally the same inside. And I knew that, even when very young. It was an incredible sense of communion. There was always that message—you're going to be OK, you're going to do something important—that I had a mission in life."

I asked Laura how she got these messages. "Not in words, I suppose?" Her answer struck me as quite beautiful:

It was a self-sense. My heart just felt expanded. It was a feeling of love, and of knowingness. A deeper perception that was communicating to me through that porthole of knowingness. Oftentimes I am called to sit and listen. It might be a tree, it might be a chickadee. I have wild chickadees around. I just sit and listen, my mind just kind of opens. One chickadee gave me this basic message: "Don't look at me as just this small, helpless bird, because there is this great message that I have to communicate to you. There is a point in your mind where your world and mine join as one, and we are brothers and sisters. We are alike, one and the same. We're not different, we're not separate. It is only the eyes, and the mind behind the eyes, that feels a duality. You understand what I communicate to you, although no spoken words are said."

I asked Laura how ordinary people can develop this power of communication.

"The first thing is the desire," she replied. "Secondly, go to a quiet place, not bombarded with other minds, other distractions. Thirdly, experience the liveness of whatever you want to contact. Take it in as much as you can. If it's a bird, feel it, feel the feathers, feel it as life, feel it as relating to the air. If it's a flower, feel the warmth of the sun, smell the smell. Allow your senses to be transsensory. Let your mind open to whatever you might be perceiving, with nonjudgment, without censoring, just allowing what comes to you. You might have a notebook and pen and just jot down whatever flows through you."

I asked Laura, "If you're working with a tree, what sort of reaction might you get?"

She replied, "Often a tree has a lot to do with relating information about what I'm going through, and why I'm going through it. I might be going through an emotional turmoil. Then the message will be very comforting, very loving, very supportive. It may tell me I'm going through this experience because it's preparing me, or it may also be a message of power, or it's an experience I have to go through as an initiation.

"I often have had the experience of a tree taking me on a journey, of going into the hollow of the tree, being met with other beings and brought into other realms. It's a question of shifting consciousness to another realm altogether. You are open to other life-forms. You can be experiencing not only the tree, but other intelligences that live in the tree, or underneath the tree, or in the roots of the tree. I'm actually talking about things that we hear about—fairies, elves, gnomes.

"It's not just the tree and the rock and the flowers that I experience, but I'm brought into their world beyond this human physical form. In becoming aware of the intelligences behind the flowers, I've met with nature spirits. There are other kingdoms that most people don't know about, where there is sacred knowledge held by some of these beings."

What a fascinating way to live, I thought. I certainly envied Laura. I mentioned to her something that Nancy Regalmuto once told me. About five years ago, Nancy was in a horrendous auto crash and suffered a head injury. Temporarily, her psychic powers disappeared. Fortunately, they returned. She told me, "For a month, all I was aware of was this physical plane. All my mystical awareness seemed to be canceled out. I thought, Is this the way 'normal' people live? How boring!"

"Yes," Laura replied, "I wouldn't allow myself to be caught on this one level. I'm just so thrilled and delighted that I can relate to other realms."

Apropos of what Laura was saying, Penelope Smith sums up her conception of nature spirits in her book, *Animals . . . Our Return to Wholeness*. She writes:

> Living beings are a composite of forms, an amalgam of spirit. There is the individual spirit in charge of a body, known as the identity or I, usually given a name by humans. There is spirit infusing every cell, every particle, every minute life form. There are the nature spirits who assist all living beings and natural environments to keep form and function growing and changing in orderly progression.
>
> The spirits of nature have various ethereal forms and functions and are known by different names or identities, according to the cultural background of those that perceive them. They are called plant spirits, flower fairies, sprites, elves, gnomes, leprechauns, landscape or mountain devas, angels. They dwell in the woods, seashores, deserts, waterways, gardens, earth, and air that have not been dispirited by human pollution or other desecration. You can communicate with the individual spirit inhabiting a tree, a flower, a rock, a mountain, and also with the attendant spirits who assist the functioning of the physical forms or areas. (pp. 311–12)

Carol Gurney of Agoura, California, had this to say about the burgeoning of animal communication:

> The movement is exploding now, and I think one of the reasons is that so many people are beginning to get back to nature. People want to find out more about animals, and the call is so strong because animals and nature represent our spirituality. I feel that we've operated from just a part of who we are—our mentality, our intellect. And that's such a small part of who we are. We can no longer survive living in such a small part of who we are. It's time that we look at the whole of who we are.
>
> It's coming out all over. In the medical field, what is Deepak Chopra talking about? He's talking about the spirit, he's talking about the

mind-body, and that we must again open that door to who we really are. He talks about meditating, and getting to know yourself on the spiritual level. Because that's where healing comes from, and animals represent that, for animals and nature are the spiritual aspect of who we are, and they've just been sitting there waiting for us to recognize that. We're here to wake up—it is time to wake up. People are awakening; they want to know who their animals really are. But the bottom line is that they want to know who they themselves are, because animals are a reflection of us.

Sean Ebnet of Ferndale, Washington, is an animal communicator who is first of all a scientist. He is a wildlife zoologist, but uses his psychic ability in conjunction with a scientific approach. "I concentrate on doing things as a biologist," he told me. "I do get messages from animals, but I have to be careful about how I include these in my reports, because I'm a scientist and I'm dealing with scientists."

However, his two professional lives often do blend together. Sometimes he uses animal communication to augment his scientific observations and data.

"I sometimes hear words from wild creatures," he told me, "but contacting wild animals is a different type of communication. You're not dealing with an animal that is domestically bred to serve people. They don't have much interaction with people, and what interaction they do have isn't particularly enjoyable. So it's difficult to get validation. You can give information to the animal, but he might not say anything back to you, and it takes two to talk. They have a different lifestyle."

I asked Sean if he has had contact with trees.

"No," he said, "I haven't tried trees. But many people whom I respect say they contact trees. Everything has frequency, everything has energy. That's why people wear crystals around their necks, that's why they hug trees and talk to plants. But as far as pictures or words, I don't get that from plants. But a plant will give off a type of light, or energy, a frequency that people can communicate with. It isn't as though you can sit down and have a conversation with a rock, but you can feel the vibrations, you're influenced by the energy. With animals, there's a frequency where you can communicate visually, another where you can communicate emotionally, and another where you can communicate physically. And of course this is also true of people communicating with each other."

Since he has worked in zoos, Sean was an intriguing source of information about the animals there—animals who are wild but not wild.

"Many of these wild animals in a domesticated setting are filled with rage," he said, "but some actually learn to enjoy it. It's kind of an individual thing. Some zoo animals become quite adept at doing nonverbal language. Sometimes you notice a change as time goes on. For example, porpoises and primates, they'd start with images and get into language. They would develop, and they'd tune in more and more to people. You'd get words, images, and feeling from the animals."

Sean may be a scientist, but he had a refreshingly mystical explanation for the translation of words from the minds of animals to the consciousness of humans, namely angels.

"You get words, images, and feeling from the animals," he said. "With words, I think it's an angel on my shoulder, translating for me. The angel takes the information and feeds it to me so I can understand it. I don't go around telling people this; they'd think I'm nuts. But it's true, that's just what it is."

———

I first heard of the fabulous sex life of slugs from Morgan Jurdan, a communicator who lives in Amboy, Washington. If it isn't true, it should be. Morgan had her first insight into the passionate slugs while she was taking a workshop from the redoubtable Penelope Smith.

"The other students," Morgan said, "had brought animals with them, but I hadn't. So Penelope said to go out and contact whatever I saw in the morning, and I contacted a slug. People in the Northwest are very conscious of slugs, and think they're awful. But they are one of the most sensuous beings I've ever connected with. They're really into their bodies and feeling, and sensing their entire environment. They're very aware of the temperature around them, the feeling of everything—the wind, fragrances. It was really wonderful.

"I was scared to share it in the circle, because everybody else had talked to dogs and cats. People sort of laughed when I said slug. But Penelope loves slugs; she's written about them in one of her books. She wrote about their great sex life. She knows everything about them, how differently colored they are, for example. They are very interesting, fascinating creatures."

I had talked with Penelope and she had sent me two of her books. In *Animals . . . Our Return to Wholeness*, I found the following fascinating paragraphs on slugs, as described by Penelope, a human being who is esteemed for permeating the consciousness of all sorts of beings:

> In the process of transporting up to 100 or so slugs each week one summer I became very close to their ways of being. I have found them to be gentle, sensitive creatures with flowing and aesthetically acute perceptions of the world. In stepping into their viewpoint, I have seen a world pulsating with waves of energy. They don't seem to see with the same kind of visual receptors as we do. They sense waves of energy, auras, so that other creatures are "shaped" according to their body form, including the energy that is emanating from their bodies. We appear to slugs as more amorphous than solid—bands of heat and colored patterns with sharp or smooth energy projections that our movements and intentions create.
>
> Slugs hear or feel sound vibrations throughout their whole bodies. Every pore in their flexible forms is sensitized to give a feeling-picture of the world. They are supremely sensuous—the gourmands of the animal world and the ultimate teachers of experiencing eating and sexual activity as fully as possible. They totally become one with their food and envelop it gracefully and lovingly into their being, whether it be tender leaves or dog excrement.
>
> I was digging in the garden and uncovered two slugs mating in a pile of leaves. Slugs are hermaphroditic, so they easily find a mate! [This reminds me of Woody Allen's immortal one-liner, "Being bisexual doubles your chances for a date on Saturday night."—Author] Contradicting the common human conception that sex is a strictly mechanical affair to animals, the slugs were intertwined in what I could feel as ecstatic communion. I respectfully covered them again. Several days later I ruffled the mulch to see if they were there, and they were still engaged in mating—obviously a pleasurable affair not to be rushed. Again, I felt their intimacy, their joy in communion, their orgasmic oneness.
>
> Slugs and other creatures that are very unlike humans physically and mentally may be hard for people to think of as intelligent and

aware. It takes getting past stereotypes and prejudices and communicating, becoming one with them in feeling and understanding, to see the beauty in their expression of life. We expand when we embrace other creatures' ways of sensing and thinking. (pp. 7–8)

Patty Breed of Stuart, Florida, says she has been communing with animals and trees since she was a child, but it's only in recent years that she has been fully aware of what she was doing. This conscious perception came about through a Christmas present from her daughter-in-law.

"It was three hours' time with an animal psychic, Kate Reilly," Patty relates. "A woman I had met casually in Hawaii had just given me a book by Penelope Smith. It seems so coincidental that these two things would happen to me, but nothing happens by mistake. I came to this late, considering that I do have this kind of talent."

Patty is not a child of the country, or even the suburbs. She was brought up in New York City, the glass and stone Big Apple. She majored in radio and television at the University of Houston, and she had a professional TV career. This is what she had to say:

Patty Breed and valued friend

I did the weather and I had a women's news show. I should have stuck with it, I could have made all that money. Later I went into retailing and then catering. Shoulda, shoulda, I shoulda done animals studies before I did, too.

I was a lonely child, and it was a lonely family. But I would talk to the trees. I've always loved trees. We lived near the Bronx Botanical Gardens, and that was my favorite place for my mother to take me. I didn't realize I was talking to trees at that time, but now I realize that's what I was doing.

I would talk to the tree in my mind, I would touch the tree, stroke the bark. The tree would almost appear to move and have a face. And be fun.

One time I was supposed to be studying for an exam, but I was not doing it. I was just sitting beside the tree, procrastinating. The tree sent me a message. It said, "All you have to do is sit still and be very quiet and it will come, you'll be able to concentrate. You can have one of my leaves to hold; that will help you concentrate."

This was a he tree. I don't know what genders they have, but it was a he tree. There was another tree that I really liked there at the gardens. I wanted a dog, and we didn't have one because we lived in the city. I was saying to the tree that I was really lonesome, and I needed someone to hug. This tree was not quite as tall as the other one, and it was kind of—I don't know what to call it, fat?—a fat tree. I think this one was a woman, and she said, "Be patient. If you'll wait, it'll come when it's supposed to come."

I didn't believe that at all, but I would keep going back to this tree. Not long after that, I did get a dog. A little dog came up to me at a horse show. The dog was going to have puppies and my mother said I could have one. So it worked.

As a child I used to talk to the furniture in my house. It was blond maple. I was very lonesome, and I would talk to this furniture, and stroke it, and it would say very comforting things to me, like, "You're not alone, you can always snuggle in me." One was a kind of over-stuffed chair, but it had a lot of wood in it. There's something about wood. Every message I ever got from a tree was very quiet and calm and solid.

I asked Patty, "Are you sure this wasn't the imagination of a lonely child?"

"I don't think that now," she replied, "not after doing workshops on animal communication with Kate Reilly, and talking with other people's animals. I write down everything I hear, and a lot of it doesn't make any particular sense to me. But then I tell it back to the owner, or whoever is the animal's person, and they'll say, 'Yes, that's right! How could you have known that?'

"I was so skeptical at first, I thought it was my imagination. But now I realize it's not."

Patty lives part of the year in Maine. She is a friend of Phil Roberts and his wife, Dinny Thorndike. She boards her horse with them. She told me of a day when she and Dinny were riding their horses along a forest trail, and they talked with a crow. I spent an afternoon with Dinny and Patty in Florida and they told me about that particular adventure.

"While we were riding along," Dinny said, "there was this crow. It was sitting so close we could have touched it. I was ahead of Patty, and I said, 'Look at that, sitting there on a branch.'"

"There was this crow on a branch," Patty said, "about the height of my horse's head. As we rode by, I heard it say, 'I don't need any help.'"

"You could hear that in your head?" I asked.

"Oh, absolutely," Patty replied, "plain as day. I said to Dinny, 'I wonder if he's OK.' And she said, 'Keep talking.'

"I said, 'Well, I'll be happy to help you if you need help.' And he said, 'No, people interfere too much a lot of times. I just need to take care of myself.'

"So I said, 'OK, I respect that. But we'll be coming back this way if you change your mind and you need help.'

"So we continued on our ride, and later on we saw him again and he said, 'I'm OK, I just needed to rest. I was really tired and I was a little disoriented.' That's what I got.

"He had contacted me; I've found a lot of animals will do that. It has to do with your aura or something. In a workshop I took, I learned a sort of formula on how to contact animals. But it seems you don't have to do that very much, they kind of like to offer, once you seem to be in the system."

I asked Patty to describe the formula she had learned.

"You get very quiet," she said. "You call the animal's name, or some identification. You send a picture of yourself. You say, 'I'd like to talk with you today, I have some things I'd like to ask you.' You ask questions. And when you're all through it's very important to say, 'Thank you very much.' You say, 'You were very helpful, you're beautiful, I admire you.' You honor the animal."

Patty and Dinny also told me about an experience they'd had in Maine with seals.

"We were out in a boat," Patty said. "We were near a reef that was filled with seals, a whole colony of them. We got the message from them that they knew the boat, that they always liked to talk with people. I took notes. One of them said, 'I'm the leader. When the boat slows, we always jump in the water because we don't know who's coming. We watch.'

"They said there was a person on the boat who thought communicating telepathically—psychically—was evil. He thought it was the work of the Devil. There *was* on the boat a person who was a religious fundamentalist. The leader seal said, 'There's something not right with the energy.'"

The seal's implication seemed to be that there might be difficulty in communicating.

I have been interested in the psychic, the intuitive, the spiritual—whatever you want to call it—for almost thirty years, and I have run across this concept a number of times. For example, the famed Israeli mystic, Uri Geller, once was stymied on a national TV program when he was interviewed along with a notorious skeptic, a show business magician. I have heard that the negative attitude of the magician prevented even this extraordinary psychic from functioning.

I ran into this principle when I first became interested in the psychic. I had met a woman named Charlotte Clarke, who was a powerful medium. This was all new to me. During a seance with half a dozen people, a seated woman began bending over backward until she was almost parallel with the floor. Charlotte began shouting, "Get out, get out, you're not welcome!" And the woman straightened up. Afterward, I asked Charlotte what that was all about. She said that the woman was a natural medium, and that she was being possessed by a spirit. Later, Charlotte called the woman at home, telling her that she was gifted psychically and that she should develop her gift. In fact, Charlotte said, she would work with her for no charge. They made an appointment. Charlotte invited me to sit in.

The woman showed up at the appointed time, but to our surprise she had brought her husband along. He was an engineer or manager, as I recall. He seemed very wary of what was going on. Nothing seemed to happen during the session; even I could tell that. When they were leaving, the man asked if there were any charge. Charlotte said yes, and quoted him a price. Afterward, I expressed surprise that she had charged him. "I thought this was going to be free," I said.

"Not for him," Charlotte said. "He invited himself. He was trying to cover up. At some level, of which he might or might not have been aware, he was thwarting the whole procedure. He was willing it not to work, and it didn't. He was terrified that his wife would be able to read his mind—his reason being that he is carrying on an affair. Let him pay for my wasted time."

However, back in Maine, the seals didn't seem to be having too much trouble communicating with the people on the boat, even though one of the passengers had a negative attitude.

In fact, according to Patty, the seal said, "Come back often. We like to look at you as much as you like to look at us. Everybody should learn how to sunbathe."

To which Patty replied, "But we get burned."

"We don't understand burned," the seal said.

At this point Patty said that the humans on the boat were going to eat lunch.

The seal responded, "That's all right, I'm going to cool off in the water. I wet myself; if you did that maybe you wouldn't get burned."

Later, another seal, swimming far on the other side of the boat, contacted Patty and said, "I'd like to talk some more about sunbathing. The sun warms our souls. Everyone needs to be warmer with each other. This bathing is just symbolic. I don't mean to be so serious, I just want you to know about being warm with each other."

Patty said that this seal also mentioned that there was something wrong with the energy. "He just didn't feel comfortable with this person on the boat," she said.

Despite the seals' apparent discomfort, they were able to carry on a whimsical dialogue:

Patty: I think your faces are so cute.
Seal: We like to look at your faces, too, but we don't think they're all cute. There is something funny about them, something comes off.
Patty: You mean hats?
Seal: You mean part of your head comes off?
Patty: No, not exactly.
Seal: This is fun; come again.

The day before I visited Patty and Dinny, they had gone to Sea World, in Orlando. They had many stories. Here is one Patty told about dolphins:

There were a lot of people around, and I didn't get much for a long time. Then one dolphin came by and said, "Can you swim belly up? Watch."

They had just been going around and around. I asked, "Can you change direction?" And they did, about three or four of them. Psttt, they went the other way. I asked, "Are you comfortable here?" One of them said, "We wish we could go deeper. The water is cool enough, but sometimes it's hard to rest."

One of them said, "We have numbers, do you want to see my number?"

It was 105. There is a lot of talk about numbers, because that's the way the keepers identify them for feeding and other things.

Dinny added that there were other species to whom numbers were significant. "The flamingos also talked about numbers. They knew they had numbers and that the numbers were important."

I asked how the dolphins felt about being in captivity, and Patty said they did not seem unhappy. She talked with one dolphin about the waters off Maine.

"But it's very far," Patty said.

"We can swim very far," the dolphin said.

"You'd be free," Patty said.

"Would anybody scratch us?" the dolphin asked.

A dolphin came by and said, "Here I am, upside down again."

———————

When I interviewed well-known animal communicator Carol Gurney, she had just returned from leading a group on a trip to Florida to swim with dolphins. She told me:

I had worked with dolphins before but only telepathically, not in the water. There was a main theme in what the dolphins were communicating. The theme was that they very much appreciated our recognizing them as teachers, as evolved beings. But they hoped we would not forget it when we left. When you are with dolphins, they open your heart chakra. You begin to feel the joy, the love, the playfulness. The dolphins want us to remember how childlike we are. We get so bloody serious, you know, and so mental about things. We forget about playing. They wanted us to recognize the beauty and love and playfulness that we see in the dolphins, to see that in ourselves and in each other. They say that we forget how to play. And that we forget that each of us and each of our animals have probably at one time been dolphins. So that when you go home to your cat or horse, or whatever you have, go with that same sense of gratitude and love in your heart to them. So that you see the same sense of grandness in your own dog and your own cat.

The dolphins asked us to swim in a circle, in a formation, and to see the beauty in each of us and to touch each other's hearts, the way they do. This was in wide-open seas. They usually come around the boat twice a day. When they come, you jump in with them. They will swim right next to you. They want you to play with them, they swirl and they turn. They'll emit their sounds to you, and you get that vibration.

I don't think anybody is really the same after they leave the dolphins. If there are any imbalances that you have, shortly thereafter they will start coming up, so that you can see the things that you're holding onto that don't serve you anymore, things that are keeping you away from being childlike, keeping you from your own sense of growth and responsibility.

When Marta Williams of Graton, California, began to study animal communication, she worked with Penelope Smith and Carol Gurney. "I learned a lot from them," she told me. "I learned the basics from Penelope. I consider myself sort of an apprentice/colleague of Carol. I've learned so much from her."

When I interviewed Marta, she had also just returned from a dolphin trip in Florida. Here is what she told me:

Carol's trip was really hard because of the weather, but our trip was really great. We had great weather and lots of dolphins. The woman who runs the trips is Rebecca Fitzgerald, who operates out of Santa Fe.

At one point we had forty dolphins in the water with us. We were out in the middle of the Bermuda Triangle on a boat for five days. The weather was gorgeous, it was just like paradise. I taught people who wanted to learn about telepathy. Not everybody was interested. With the people who were, we got to a place where everybody was getting it and communicating with the dolphins, and we did a lot of work toward getting some real personal information from the dolphins.

My conclusions are that dolphins are really master healers, and they have decided to try to heal the earth and heal people. That's what they want to do on this planet as a group. They work by laying down energy lines in the ocean, trying to readjust and rebalance the earth. And they also heal people with their sound and also by physically bumping into them, touching them.

And we noticed on the boat, a lot of us, that we were going through really huge emotional changes. They caused us to go through emotional changes that are really healing. That's one thing I would say for sure about them. They are really highly evolved; they are amazingly powerful animals.

I wanted to ask them, are you so evolved that you're martyrs? People have told me that dolphins don't care if they die, they're just doing this for the betterment of the planet, for the highest good. So I asked them, and they said, "We don't like to go through pain and suffering. What happens to us is a consequence of the work we've chosen to do." But animals are much better at understanding that death is not permanent, that they can come back. It's not so traumatic for them to die.

I think everybody on the ship got a real personal message from the dolphins. One or two of the dolphins would single them out and come back every day to be with them. It was amazing, just amazing.

When I was writing books about ghosts, I made every effort to find witnesses and other available corroboration for each case. I would be particularly impressed—even rather pleased—when spirits would invade my workroom and move or remove objects—a film roll, a sheaf of research, a finished chapter in a manuscript. They would garble tapes and phone calls. Parapsychological wisdom—some scoffers would say that is a contradiction in terms—has it that spirits who are hanging about the physical plane have a desire to get the attention of us mortals. They certainly got mine over a period of years. But to me these were not unwelcome experiences. They were firsthand. I was not dependent on anyone else's word; they had happened to me. It was reasonable proof to me that there were other inhabited dimensions around, even though I couldn't see or hear what might be going on there.

Sometimes I would run across a case that depended on the subjective experience—and the word—of one person. And occasionally, if the story were intriguing enough, I would include it in a book, with the caveat to the reader to believe it or not. I offer that caveat to you, dear reader, with regard to the following account. It was given to me by Kate Solisti, whose adventures with trees and rocks also appear in this chapter. Kate is a very convincing person—educated, cultured, spiritual— with an apparently complete set of marbles. I asked her if she had had psychic communication with wild animals, and she said she had had telepathic long-distance connection with elephants. Here is her story:

> I guess that I always thought that elephants were special, and I decided to reach out to them and see what they wanted to share with me. I didn't know what to ask. I just asked if there was anything they'd like to tell me, and this beautiful stuff came through.
>
> The elephant is a very special being. The elephant has a sisterhood of singers with the whales. They are singing constantly to the Mother Earth. All of the elephants are singers. Scientists have discovered recently that elephants are constantly vocalizing, but it's usually at a decibel that the human ear cannot hear—it's too low. What is important about that is the whales vocalize where we can hear them but also way above—as well as below—where we can hear. This is very important, because elephants have told me that they and the whales set the *basso continuo*.

"Which means?" I asked.

"In the Baroque period," she replied, "it was customary for the composer to write a simple line, and then all the instrumentalists improvised around it. The bass line becomes the constant in the symphony. The elephants and the whales weave songs and sounds that are extraordinarily rich and multifaceted. The elephants told me that they and the whales sing this line that balances the planet, and that all the other species on the planet sing their songs in and around it."

This was intriguing stuff; I urged Kate to continue. She said:

> Humans also have a song to sing. We don't do it very often, unfortunately. Some of us do it, but most of us have forgotten it. It's an energetic sound—it's a sound and it's beyond a sound.
>
> The important thing about the elephants is that they sing to the Mother Earth, and without them there would be a great problem. If we were to lose the elephant, there would be a huge imbalance set up on the planet. The humpback are the major singers among the whales, and they weave a sound in the ocean that is the counterpart of the elephant's song on land.

Pat Wilson of Beverly, Massachusetts, is a devotee of elephants and whales, and has a substantial collection of books and articles about them. Although none of it involved the spiritual, mystical cast that we are talking about in this book, it was interesting information. For example:

From *Friends of the Ocean*, a brochure: "Studies have shown that humpback whales sing true songs that are composed of an ordered sequence of musical sounds, much like a songbird. Their song is made up of six themes, repeated over and over again. Each song can last up to 35 minutes, with a definite beginning and end, and may form part of a much longer recital."

From *National Geographic*: "Beluga [whales] travel in a capsule of wild sounds, their lives spent in a symphony orchestra tuning up. A deep tuba voice blares through the air, followed by a long, wavering tone like a novice sounding a trumpet. Then a series of high trilling chirps and the sibilant sound of exhaled air, a blatt, a snore. One can hear a cascade of clicks."

A forbidding note from *National Geographic*: "A survey makes grim reading about how elephants are being sacrificed for their tusks. . . . We develop the land, forcing earth's largest terrestrial mammal . . . to the brink of extinction. After shooting many of Africa's largest tuskers, poachers have turned their guns on young elephants with smaller tusks, speeding the slaughter. For each ton of ivory, poachers shot nearly twice as many elephants in 1988 as in 1979."

I spoke with two animal communicators about the information that Kate Solisti had imparted, and they were both in concurrence with her views. One is Barbara Janelle of London, Ontario, who has a master's degree in medical geography, which is akin to epidemiology. She has taught geography at the University of Colorado and the University of Western Ontario. She said, "Yes, animals sing songs, songs that can be heard and songs our human ears don't catch. The song strikes a balance. My experience is that all creatures, from earthworms right on up, have songs. They contribute to the health of all creatures, whether animals or

Barbara Janelle and Houdini

trees, and we can extend this to rocks. It's like a worldwide web. I agree totally with what Kate Solisti has to say, and it's beautifully put."

Barbara also spoke of the unheard songs of humans: "With respect to humans, there's a quality in your heart's singing. It doesn't come with words; it doesn't come with sound. It's almost like a wave outward. And it's that kind of song that affects not only other beings who are near you, but it also affects the whole planet. What we're really doing is building songs for the planet. The earth opens its heart."

Another communicator, Sananjaleen, of Rectortown, Virginia, said:

The songs are like a toning, a frequency. As I understand it, this toning heals the earth. It's like we're singing to ourselves. If we were to lose the elephant there would be a great imbalance set up on the earth. In a meditation, I got this message: The elephants send a warning— pay attention to the needs of your brother. Take care before you destroy the elephant nation. The elephants were a gift to you, and as you destroy them you destroy your understanding. For as the dolphins and the whales reflect the condition of the oceans to the higher realms, so do the elephants reflect the conditions on the surface of the earth.

When man claims the elephant country for himself, so does he diminish the planet. Energy is withdrawn entirely, there will be a void, and a void is not a healthy state of affairs.

I asked Kate Solisti who sang these mystical songs among humans, and she replied, "I believe there are indigenous peoples on the planet like the Aborigines and different tribal peoples that remember the song and sing it as part of their ceremonies. The Hopi and the Zuni and the Navajo have been practicing the same ceremonies for centuries. And the Tibetans and the Eskimos, the Inuit people. It's a part of their way of life. I think Westerners are searching for the voice."

14

Are Some Animals Poets?

I saved this chapter for last.

It makes me a bit nervous, for I'm afraid it qualifies as offbeat to the fourth power—or possibly the fifth. But I feel that to ignore this aspect of my research would be abdicating my duty to both animal lovers and devotees of the psychic, not to mention unreconstructed skeptics eager to scoff, and possibly editors of the *National Enquirer* looking for material.

To get to the sticky point: I kept hearing almost from the first interview that a few animals not only speak in English prose, but sometimes come up with poetry. And judging from the poetry furnished me by the communicators involved, it is not doggerel, but good poetry.

I got my introduction to poetic animals while I was interviewing animal communicator Phil Roberts, a former dairy farmer. He was telling me about talking telepathically to cats at an animal shelter not far from his home. He mentioned casually that he had received a poem from a cat. This *really* got my attention.

My skepticism went into overdrive. "Are you sure that you didn't create this yourself—unconsciously?" I asked.

He insisted he was no poet. "I give all the credit to the cat," he said.

He read the cat's poem to me, and here it is:

> Stop and feel what the granite is telling you.
> Watch us to learn real beauty in moving and not moving.
> Move like a cat,
> Like me.
> Soften the granite, the emotions, the flow.
> Think like a cat, to gentle the words.
> Think of me soft,
> To relax the body, to ease the pain.

My next experience with a poem from an animal came during an interview with Adele Tate of Byron, Illinois. Adele, a communicator, told me about Windstan, an extraordinary horse, afflicted with a painful disease, who had agreed to be euthanized. On the day before he was to be put down, Windstan telepathically dictated to Adele a letter for his owner, about his life and death. (An account of Windstan's death is given in detail in Chapter 9.)

"He also wrote a poem," Adele told me. "I have absolutely no talent whatsoever, so I know it didn't come from me. I am totally unable to do prose or poetry. The poem was absolutely beautiful."

This is the poem Windstan gave Adele:

> Come to the field and
>   be with the wind
> Feel the warm of the sun on your hair.
> It is me who gently
>   Caresses your face
>   and tickles your cheek with a tear.
> Smile as you watch the moon chase the sun
>   and the dark takes over the light.
> It is me who gently brushes your brow
>   and kisses the tear from your eye.
> As the morning comes gently over the hill
>   and the wind now caresses your face
> It is me whom you feel
>   deep in your heart . . .
> You know we are never apart.

Sharon Lunde of Prince George, British Columbia, is an equestrienne, and runs a dressage clinic. She has a horse that she says creates poetry.

"This horse, Bonn Jovi, is just incredible," she says. And she told me the circumstances under which the poem had been given to her.

"I was in meditation with him," she said. "I was in my house sitting in my favorite chair for meditation. I talk to Bonn Jovi a lot when he's out in a barn or in a pasture, doing his thing. There had been one adversity after another, and I always sort of go to him when I feel that way. When you are an animal communicator you put out a tremendous amount of energy, so to get that energy back I go to Bonn Jovi and he gives it to me. We were sort of generalizing about what we were going to do that day. All of a sudden he said, 'I would like to give you a poem, something to brighten the day.' And he gave it to me and I wrote it down."

I asked Sharon if she had any ideas on how an animal could come up with poetry.

"That's very hard for people to grasp," she replied. "For me, it's easy, because animals come back again, they are reincarnated. So probably in a previous life Bonn Jovi was human, a sage of some kind."

I asked her if she were sure it was possible for a human to be reincarnated as an animal. "Oh yes," she said, "I am able to communicate with animals and go into their minds, and see their past lives as to what they have been, and some *have* been human."

This is Bonn Jovi's poem as Sharon gave it to me:

Tick Tock

Come ride with me
Fluid motion
One on one
Melting into time and space.
Both of us perform
With effortless grace
TIME
That looming enemy
Jump for joy!

I am a faceless clock
You, a shaft of light
Upon my back.
TIME

Our rhythmic hearts
Beat as one
TICK TOCK

Occasionally, as I wended my way through the communicator community, I would query my interviewee about animals and poetry. The reply of Sue Goodrich of Escondido, California, is typical. "Animals reincarnate, absolutely," she said. "Some have been human. That might be where the poetry comes from."

As Winterhawk, an animal communicator from Hayward, California, was describing the ways she communicates with animals—visually, emotionally, through physical sensation—she mentioned, "I'm very audio so I hear words. Sometimes animals send me poetry."

Sharon Lunde with the poetic horse, Bonn Jovi

MOTHER GOOSE & GRIMM by Mike Peters

Reprinted by permission: Tribune Media Services

Dr. Judith Shoemaker of West Grove, Pennsylvania, a very highly regarded veterinarian—she's licensed in twelve states and works with many animal communicators—told me that poetry definitely comes through animals.

"Absolutely," she said, "that's very real. There are a couple of horses in this area that actually do that. I'm a great cynic. I'm very much a scientist, with left brain beyond belief. Most surgeons are. But the neat thing about this is that there are *mechanics* to it. The mechanics of this intuitive knowledge are very real. We're all wired to do this stuff, our nervous systems are set up. Everybody is similar enough so that it is in there."

I asked her what she thought of the idea that poet animals have been humans in the past.

"That's a very interesting thought," she replied. "I'm not sure I believe that, although I know some very wise animals, animals that are wiser than people. I had some early-on ideas that animals follow a parallel spiritual evolution, but I'm not sure."

———

"I've gotten poems from my birds," communicator Mary Esther Borie of Santa Rosa, California, told me. "I have a copy of one, it's really beautiful. The bird's name is Franklin. The full name I gave him is Franklin Roosevelt, because he thinks he's so important. He's a hotshot. He's a gray-cheeked parakeet. They're very sure of themselves."

Here is the poem:

New Wings

One night as I let the stars out of my head
I flew to a distant galaxy
And there I took up a new flight
Of living without encumbrances
And letting my soul breathe with new depth.

"That's great! Give him a gold star for that one!" I urged Mary Esther.

Through Sharon Lunde, who gave me the poem from her horse, Bonn Jovi, I also received a poem from a dog, Belle, who had lived with Brenda and John Colebrooke. Sharon has often worked with the Colebrookes' animals. They live in Prince George, British Columbia.

Brenda told me, "Belle, a chocolate Lab, was aging. She was unwell, weak, wasn't eating or drinking. She told Sharon that she needed to leave her body, but was holding on because she knew I couldn't accept

Brenda Colebrooke, with Belle the poet in the center and sister Sarah on the right

her leaving at that time. Sharon gave her a healing, and she rallied to bless us with her presence for a couple more months so we could accept her leaving.

"You have no idea how Belle's poem helped me prepare, and accept the confirmation that it was time to assist Belle with leaving her body. I will share with you one of her quotations I received during our last communication, through Sharon: 'The wind moves life on; the sun dries up things and blows them away. All the elements of nature reinforce the circle of life.'"

This is Belle's poem:

> Softly, slowly,
> Don't you hear?
> Death is near
> The force so strong.
> Bren, I can't hold on.
> The wind, it's tugging,
> Pulling me along,
> The force is too strong.
> Softly, slowly,
> Don't you hear?
> The gale force that was once my life
> Is now a gentle breeze.
> Let me go with the wind,
> Let me sail, let me fly,
> I do not die.

———

Penelope Smith, possibly the best known of current animal communicators and teachers of the craft, is a poet in her own right, and includes her poetry throughout her book *Animals . . . Our Return to Wholeness*. She also includes poetry from animals, in one case from her Afghan hound, Popiya. She writes that in doing counseling with Popiya after the dog had had a seizure she found that Popiya had, in a former life as a Jewish boy, died in a German concentration camp. Penelope writes in her book:

In the course of counseling Popiya, I discovered that I had known her when she was the young German boy. I was an Austrian Jewish man, and we had crossed paths on a truck taking us to the concentration camps. She had shared some of her poetry with me on the way. In her Afghan form, Popiya dictated a series of haunting poems of her feelings from that life and her struggles to come to terms with herself, which I call "The Popiya Series."

The first section of the poetry, dated 23 January 1978, is as follows:

> I am alone in my vision
> And the breeze that haunts me
> Is of ages past
> Friends gone
> Poems lost in the wind.
> Brutality claimed my art
> My gift to the world
> Of rhyme and gentle song.
>
> I caress the day and the sun
> In this warm land
> Where comfort and love
> Ease my mind and coax my tongue
> Once again to reach out
> To dare to be myself.
>
> Through my friend
> My words are written
> I ask in quietness
> Edging from my sorrow
> To have them heard.
>
> I am again here
> Peering softly from my hiding
> To say hello.
> My tears speak
> My joy from wells below the pain
> Is touched and aches
> To touch you, too.

Hello, I want to say
Do not speak loudly
Caress me gently with your smile
And let me put my head
Close to your hand or foot
I am here again
Hello.

Marta Williams of Graton, California, is one of those people I love to talk with for purposes of this book—she's a scientist. She has degrees in biology and ecology from the University of California at Berkeley and from San Francisco State University. Although she is a practicing animal communicator, she still works part-time in the environmental consulting field. I asked her for some thoughts concerning linguistic communication with animals. I mentioned that someone along the way had expressed the opinion that animals who have lived in people's

Penelope Smith, with Reya the Afghan; photo by Marty Knapp

MOTHER GOOSE & GRIMM by Mike Peters

Reprinted by permission: Tribune Media Services

houses have quite a vocabulary, and it is perhaps these animals—or reincarnations of them—who write poetry. Marta replied:

> My opinion is that *all* animals have quite a vocabulary, and it's not a matter of their learning it. My understanding of telepathy and the way I experience it is that it's a universal language, that you have instant translation. So whatever concepts they're trying to give you, you can receive. Animals are totally intelligent, just like we are. The difference is that they communicate in a different language than we do. We communicate verbally and audibly. But the *universal* language is telepathy. I think that many years ago, maybe thousands of years, we were all telepathic with each other, and we've just lost it. It's kind of like a trip to paradise to find it again. The reason animals can talk to you is that they are totally sentient beings, just like we are. There's something like a universal force that is instantaneously translating their thoughts and feelings and what they want to communicate to us into something we can understand. So if I'm German, I'm going to understand it in German. It'll be in German and I'll hear German words. If I'm English, I'll hear English words. It just happens, it's there, it's a great gift and we don't have to worry about it.

I told Marta that so far in my travels among communicators I had heard of a cat and a horse who communicated in poetry.

Marta: I know this sounds crazy, but I have a newt who does this.
Author: A what?
Marta: I raised some newts from eggs. I got them from somebody who owned a fish store.

Author: The only newt I know of is Newt Gingrich.

Marta: My comment on Newt Gingrich is that he gives newts a bad name.

Author: What *are* newts?

Marta: They're like salamanders and they have an orange belly and they're real cute. One of my newts actually wrote one poem. He hasn't done any more, but he did write one poem.

Author: How do you figure that would happen?

Marta: Well, one of the things that we who work with animals a lot, who do a lot of telepathy with them, find out is that . . . and you've got to open up your mind to this . . .

Author: Sure.

Marta: The religious fundamentalists are not going to go for this . . .

Author: So what?

Marta: . . . but we have found out that animals really reincarnate.

Author: Yeah, I was about to bring that up.

Marta: So I firmly believe that this newt must have been a person who wrote poetry at one time or another.

Marta Williams and Brydie. Marta, an ecologist, would like it noted that the bushes in the background are California blackberries.

Author: I talked with this fellow up in Maine who told me about a cat who had given him a poem, but he wasn't too hip on how the cat could have done it. He only knew that he couldn't have written it himself. He seems to be a really good animal communicator. He's an expert. He can do it, but doesn't know how he does it. I myself am a typical journalist, I learn a lot about a thing superficially, I just can't *do* it.

Marta: Arthur, you've got to start saying, "Yeah, I *can* do it!"

Same to you, dear reader.

Arthur Myers; photo by Virginia Cutler

Appendix A

Further Reading

Barlow, Dennis. *Psychic Animals*. New York: Henry Holt and Company, 1987.

Boone, J. Allen. *Kinship with All Life*. New York: Harper & Row, 1954.

Lydecker, Beatrice. *What the Animals Tell Me*. New York: Harper & Row, 1977.

Roads, Michael J. *Talking with Nature*. Tiburon, CA: H. J. Kramer, Inc., 1985.

Smith, Penelope. *Animal Talk*. Point Reyes, CA: Pegasus Publications, 1989.

————. *Animals . . . Our Return to Wholeness*. Point Reyes, CA: Pegasus Publications, 1993.

Tellington-Jones, Linda. *The Tellington TTouch*. New York: Viking, 1992.

Thomas, Elizabeth Marshall. *The Hidden Life of Dogs*. Boston: Houghton Mifflin Co., 1993.

Wright, Machaelle Small. *Behaving as if the God in All Life Mattered*. Jeffersonton, VA: Perelanda, Ltd., 1983.

Appendix B

Professional Animal Communicators

Western United States

Mary Esther Borie
2020 Midway Dr.
Santa Rosa, CA 95405
(707) 544-1652

Consultations. Instruction for individuals. Energy healing.

Sean Ebnet
5026 Elder Rd.
Ferndale, WA 98248
(360) 380-1297

Consultations, lectures, and workshops. Specializes in sports equine work, massage.

Sue Goodrich
1205 Bear Valley Parkway
Escondido, CA 92027
(619) 480-2474

Consultations, lectures, and workshops. Reiki, TTouch, Jin Shin Jyutsu, Bach flowers, and nutrition.

Carol Gurney
3714 N. Cornell Rd.
Agoura, CA 91301
(818) 597-1154

Workshops, lectures, and consultations.

Morgan Jurdan
1135 Yale Bridge Rd.
Amboy, WA 98601
(206) 247-5310

Consultations and workshops. Reiki healing, flower essences, and nature healing.

Samantha Khury
1251 10th St.
Manhattan Beach, CA 90266
(310) 374-6812

Consultations, workshops, and lectures. Audiotapes and videotapes.

Sam Louie
P.O. Box 14741
Berkeley, CA 94742
(510) 644-1583

Consultations, lectures, and workshops. Massage.

Raphaela Pope
P.O. Box 14741
Berkeley, CA 94712
(510) 548-4550

Consultations, lectures, and workshops. Reiki and TTouch.

Jeri Ryan
P.O. Box 10166
Oakland, CA 94610
(510) 653-6609 or
(510) 569-6123

Lectures, consultations, and workshops. Reiki treatment. Spiritual healings.

Penelope Smith
P.O. Box 1060
Point Reyes, CA 94956
(415) 663-1247

A pioneer in the field. Books, audiotapes, and videotapes. Lectures and workshops. Not available for private consultations.

Kate Solisti-Mattelon
5807 S. Reed Way #1416
Littleton, CO 80123
(303) 734-1247

Consultations.

Teresa Wagner
P.O. Box 522
Monterey, CA 93942
(408) 375-9389

Consultations. Specializes in issues surrounding euthanasia, death, loss, and grief. Workshops in grieving the loss of animals.

Marta Williams
P.O. Box 110
Graton, CA 95444
(707) 829-8186

Consultations, workshops, and individual tutoring.

Winterhawk
P.O. Box 56065
Hayward, CA 94545-6065
(510) 538-7763

Consultations, lectures, and workshops. Animal spirit contacts and healings; flower essences; blue-green algae.

Southwestern United States

Becky Ferris
461 Cheryl Ave.
White Rock, NM 87544
(505) 672-3920

Consultations, lectures, and workshops.

Griffin Kanter
5223 Arboles Dr.
Houston, TX 77035
(713) 728-4985

Consultations, lectures, and workshops. Bach flower remedies. Reiki master.

Judy Meyers
Route 4, Box 57-J
Santa Fe, NM 87501
(505) 820-7387

Is not now doing private consultations but will provide information on how to get such service.

Midwestern United States

Tim Beihoff
North 82, West 22371
Sandra Dr.
Sussex, WI 53089
(414) 251-6548

Consultations; specializes in finding lost animals.

Marcia Ramsland
Box 5
Saginaw, MN 55779
(218) 729-6479

Consultations and lectures.

Laura Simpson
704 East Burlington
Fairfield, IA 52556-3127
(515) 472-3604

Consultations; specializes in finding lost animals.

Jacquelin Smith
5795 North Meadows Blvd. #B
Columbus, OH 43229
(614) 436-8831

Lectures, workshops, Bach flower remedies, and chakra balancing.

Adele Tate
4445 Walden Rd.
Byron, IL 61010
(815) 234-5787

Consultations and workshops.

Donetta Zimmerman
5814 Lathrop Pl.
Cincinnati, OH 45224

Consultations.

Eastern United States

Anita Curtis
P.O. Box 182
Gilbertsville, PA 19525
(610) 327-3820

Consultations, lectures, and workshops.

Gloria Glossbrenner
Rt. #1, Box 305
Bealton, VA 22712
(703) 439-0312

Consultations, workshops combining communication with horse riding instruction, and Reiki healing.

Dawn Hayman
3364 State Route 12
Clinton, NY 13323

Lectures, workshops, and consultations.

Denise Kinch
118 King St.
Groveland, MA 01834

Consultations and lectures.

Betty Lewis
17 Danbury Circle
Amherst, NH 03031
(603) 673-3263

Consultations, lectures, and workshops. TTouch, Reiki, and Bach flowers.

Barbara Meyers
29 Lyman Ave.
Staten Island, NY 10305
(718) 720-5548

Consultations; specializes in grief therapy.

Nancy Regalmuto
18 Woodland Park Rd.
Bellport, NY 11713
(516) 286-1057

Consultations, workshops, and lectures; specializes in physical and behavioral holistic therapy.

Kate Reilly
1511 N. Lafayette St.
Shelby, NC 28150
(704) 482-2018

Consultations, workshops, and lectures. Healing through attunement of the energy field.

Phil Roberts Jr.
RFD #1, Box 5375
Lincolnville, ME 04849
(207) 763-3453

Consultations; specializes in animal behavior problems.

Sananjaleen
P.O. Box 222
Rectortown, VA 22140
(540) 364-1282

Workshops; specializes in advice concerning the transition period.

Marlene Sandler
P.O. Box 476
Warrington, PA 18976
(215) 491-0707

Workshops, lectures, consultations, and Reiki healing and attunements.

Janet Shepherd
1707 Mercer Rd.
Haymarket, VA 22069
(703) 754-8335

Consultations.

Laura Silva   Consultations, workshops, and lectures.
262 Tom Swamp Rd.
Petersham, MA 01366
(508) 249-0997

Jan Spiers   Consultations and workshops.
15553 Hardwick Mountain
Gordonsville, VA 22942
(540) 832-3456

Melanie Thompson   Consultations, lectures, and workshops.
HC74, Box 147
East Baldwin, ME 04024
(207) 787-2496

Nedda Wittels   Telepathic communication, lectures,
9 Knollwood Circle   and workshops. Hands-on healing.
Simsbury, CT 06070
(203) 651-5771

Jim Worsley   Consultations, lectures, and workshops.
6806 Edmonstone Circle   Also does rebirthing.
Richmond, VA 23226
(804) 285-8936

Canada

Barbara Janelle   Consultations and lectures. TTouch.
169 Duchess Ave.
London, Ontario N6C 1P1,
    Canada
(519) 672-5057

Sharon Lunde   Consultations by phone
SS3 C17 S34   or correspondence.
Prince George, British
    Columbia V2N 2S7,
    Canada
(604) 964-7700

Index